ST. PAU'
1
S

Thinking about Prayer

Thinking about Prayer

Owen F. Cummings

WIPF & STOCK · Eugene, Oregon

THINKING ABOUT PRAYER

Copyright © 2009 Owen F. Cummings. All rights reserved. Except for brief quotations in critical publications or reviews, no part of this book may be reproduced in any manner without prior written permission from the publisher. Write: Permissions, Wipf and Stock Publishers, 199 W. 8th Ave., Suite 3, Eugene, OR 97401.

Wipf & Stock
A Division of Wipf and Stock Publishers
199 W. 8th Ave., Suite 3
Eugene, OR 97401

www.wipfandstock.com

ISBN 13: 978-1-60608-776-3

Manufactured in the U.S.A.

For Cathy,

Companion on the journey for thirty-seven years,

I carry you in my heart.

Contents

Introduction | ix

CHAPTER ONE Prayer as Thinking | 1

CHAPTER TWO The Lord's Prayer, Challenge, and Comfort | 13

CHAPTER THREE Psalm 23 | 27

CHAPTER FOUR Praying the Rosary | 35

CHAPTER FIVE John Henry Newman's *Lead, Kindly Light* | 47

CHAPTER SIX Spirituality and the Arts | 59

CHAPTER SEVEN The Grace of Graham Greene (1904–1991) | 65

CHAPTER EIGHT The Eucharist Makes the Church | 77

CHAPTER NINE John Donne, Catholicism, and the Eucharist | 89

CHAPTER TEN P. D. James and Liturgy | 101

CHAPTER ELEVEN The Eucharist and James P. Mackey | 113

CHAPTER TWELVE Eucharistic Absence | 123

Bibliography | 135

Introduction

THIS LITTLE BOOK WANDERS far and wide through issues of prayer and worship. These issues are absolutely central to the life of Christians. The Christian life is marked by prayer and worship. These are the most obvious verifying characteristics of the active and engaged Christian. They cannot be dispensed with. At the same time, what is happening in prayer and worship is not always clear. If too hard and fast a line is drawn between those who pray and worship in their conventional confessional tradition and those who do not, all suffer. The church exists for the world. The church exists as sacrament of salvation for the world. It is not purely and simply the absolute enclave of the saved. The chapters in this book quite deliberately reach out to the active Christian. At the same time, they are directed also at those Christians who are not especially active as church. The purpose has been to broaden and deepen our understanding of prayer and worship so as to enhance the church's work of mission and evangelization. Thus, chapters 1 to 7 treat of prayer and chapters 9 to 12 reflect on the central Christian prayer, the Eucharist, but from a variety of perspectives.

Chapter 1 has to do with "Prayer as Thinking." Not all thinking is prayer but there are forms of thinking that approximate prayer and these approximations help us recognize points of contact between those who pray and those who do not. Chapters 2 and 3 deal with "The Lord's Prayer" and Psalm 23, arguably two of the best-known prayers in the Christian tradition. The chapters assist in reaching to a deeper level of understanding of them and hopefully of praying them. Chapter 3 is "Praying the Rosary." It will probably speak immediately to Catholics because of the role of the Rosary in Catholic tradition. Nevertheless, the chapter also reaches out more broadly to show that the mysteries of the Rosary speak to the living situation of Christians. Chapters 5, 6, and 7 open up larger horizons: 5 comments on Newman's poem "Lead, Kindly Light," showing its meaning not only for the author but also for us; 6 reflects on how the arts may be of assistance in both theology and spirituality; 7 attempts to show chapter 6 at work by engaging with Graham Greene's novel, *The Heart of the Matter*. Chapter 8 takes on a eucharistic pilgrimage through the first 1500 years of Christianity, showing how the Eucharist was appreciated by forebears in the faith. Chapters 9, 10, and 11 speak of particular authors and the Eucharist: 9 speaks of John Donne in the sixteenth and seventeenth centuries; 10 comments on the meaning of liturgy and Eucharist for the crime-writer P. D. James; and 10 relates to the sometimes uncomfortable Eucharistic thinking of the contemporary theologian, James P. Mackey. The final chapter attempts to comment on the meaning of Christians' absence from Sunday worship and in particular the Eucharist.

There is little in this book that will not be known to the interested Christian, but the hope is that reading it may help expand the meaning and practice of what Christians already do in praying and worshiping. The chapters originated in a series of conferences to the Trappist monks of Our Lady of Guadalupe Abbey, Lafayette, Oregon, and I owe Abbot Peter McCarthy, OCSO and the monastic community a debt of gratitude for listening to what they already knew and practiced.

CHAPTER ONE

Prayer as Thinking

If you teach the children how to pray, then you will have taught them all they really need to know in life about religion.

Sister Oswin Marsh

MANY YEARS AGO WHEN I was a younger professor of theology at Newman University College, Birmingham, England, I had a colleague in the Department of Theology, Sister Oswin Marsh, one of whose responsibilities was to teach the principles and practice of religious education to those students who were studying to become elementary school teachers. The students represented every point on the denominational spectrum, and none. With this very heterogeneous group, and perhaps as much for their advantage as for the advantage of the pupils that they would in future teach, Sister Oswin would begin her course with these words: "If you teach the children how to pray, then you will have taught them all they really need to know in life about religion." I recall thinking at the time, "How quaint! How pious! How very inadequate!" My perception was that children in a rapidly changing world, the pluralistic religious world of today, needed to know a great deal more than how to pray. Children in my judgment needed to know about the bigger religious world, the different religious traditions that lived in close proximity in the sprawling modern metropolis. They needed to know about the ritual dimension of religion, about various moral traditions, about family practices in the great world faiths around them. I suspect that Sister Oswin would have agreed. Children ought to have a comprehensive religious education to meet the needs of negotiating their way in a religiously complex world. Yet now, and perhaps this is a sign of getting older, I believe that her initial position was correct. "If you teach the children how to pray, then you will have taught them all they really need to know in life about religion." Prayer is at the heart of all religion, not just as a general principle, but as a living existential reality. At good times and in bad, in sickness and in health, with a heart full of praise and gratitude, or with a heart broken with grief and sadness, prayer takes us into the heart of God, into the heart of the divine reality.

Maturing and Praying

At the same time, it needs to be acknowledged that while prayer is at the heart of all religion, "for many Christians prayer has become something of an embarrassment." Questions may be asked, such as: "Is there a place for prayer in the kind of world in which we live, marked by science and technology? Is prayer an infantile exercise which the adult must put away?" Prayer has become something of an embarrassment for many people because, while they have grown older and have matured in the life cycle, oftentimes their way of praying has not kept pace with their maturation in life. So, prayer simply has been dropped as something one abandons as one grows up. It is a thing of childhood.

Perhaps we might say that faith develops like a tree: a tree needs nourishment and water, sunlight, and it grows by adding rings. The rings it adds are dependent on the earlier rings. The earlier rings of a tree are not simply displaced and jettisoned as the tree grows. Yet, the later rings of the tree as it continues to grow and to expand make it different in some ways.[1]

In some ways the growth of the human person in Christian faith is very similar. Initially that growth is dependent upon the nourishment and example offered by the adult environment. We might call that the accepting phase of faith, the phase most characteristic of the elementary school years. It is an imitative phase of faith. What the child sees in the parents the child puts into place for herself. There is little reflection or critique. This is the template also for praying. The child learns the

---

1. For this way of thinking, see John H. Westerhoff, III, *Will Our Children Have Faith?* rev. ed. (Harrisburg, PA: Morehouse Publishing, 2000).

prayers of childhood by repeating them after parents and teachers and by continuing to repeat them in her own life. The foundations of praying are being laid. Gradually this phase gives way to a questioning phase, as the child moves through the years of junior high and high school. The practices of childhood are now sifted and critiqued as the young person learns to think for him or herself. This is entirely good and as it should be. The young person is seeking to appropriate a worldview that she or he can call their own, and this is where things can become a little more complex when it comes to prayer. Often, a certain dissatisfaction grows with the prayer-patterns of childhood. If different prayer patterns are not entered into, then the likelihood is that prayer may be abandoned. Prayer has to fit in with who I am, and who I am in Christian faith changes and develops through the life cycle. Perhaps we might say that the final phase of development in religious faith is the mature phase. The mature phase emerges in adulthood, not without strong and firm commitment, and not without a struggle. At this stage in life, prayer has developed to meet the experience, needs and perceptions of an alert and aware adult. If prayer patterns have not kept pace with the developmental needs of a growing and maturing adult, then it is very likely that prayer will atrophy in a person's life, and may indeed vanish for the most part. Or, it may happen that a person will simply rely on the prayer patterns of childhood. In itself that is not necessarily a bad thing, because the person continues to pray, but it could be so much better. It could be so much better because the person is not a child any more. The more our lived experience can be incorporated and integrated into the fabric of our worshiping and praying lives, the more enriched and satisfying those worshiping and praying lives will be. So our concern in this chapter will be this: Is there a way of understanding prayer that will be commensurate with the growing and maturing person? I have no certitude about these matters, but I have found the following thoughts helpful in my own life of prayer, and it is out of that they are offered to the reader.[2]

Prayer as Thinking

Prayer has to do with communication with God. In prayer we open ourselves to the reality of God, consciously and with awareness. This

---

2. The influence of the Anglican theologian John Macquarrie (1919–2007) is gratefully acknowledged throughout this chapter, especially his *Paths in Spirituality*, 2nd edition (Harrisburg, PA: Morehouse Publishing, 1992).

means that prayer is a kind of thinking. This fits with the traditional Christian catechetical definition of prayer: "Prayer is a raising up of the mind and heart to God." Raising up the mind is thinking about something. Raising up the mind and heart is thinking about something with a degree of intensity, so that it is not just a cerebral experience but involves the whole person. Prayer is thinking, or perhaps better, prayer is not less than thinking. We need to make differentiations about thinking. There are different kinds of thinking, for example, the kind of thinking that goes on in science or in economics. Clearly, prayer is not that kind of thinking. It is not the pragmatic, or the clinical, or the objective kind of thinking, or even the routine kind of thinking that is all-important and upon which so much in life depends. Prayer as thinking is different. Perhaps we could say that prayer is thinking that is passionate, compassionate, responsible and thankful. Let us consider each one of these forms of thinking in turn.

By passionate thinking is intended the kind of thinking that goes beyond mechanical and routine thinking. Passionate thinking is the kind of thinking in which we are really engaged in a life-giving kind of way. This is how theologian John Macquarrie describes it: "There is a thinking that enters feelingly into the world and knows itself deeply involved in all that goes on there."[3] Passionate thinking is thinking about matters that really concern us, matters about which we feel strongly. That is passionate thinking. We are different as a result of this kind of thinking, and the difference is felt. Passionate thinking is sometimes marked by joy, sometimes by gratitude, sometimes by a great sense of sorrow especially when we have been responsible for causing sorrow to others. People may have stopped praying in any formal sense of the word, but is there anyone who does not experience passionate thinking? Passionate thinking is knit into the very fabric of what it means to be a human being.

Compassionate thinking. Compassion means opening one's heart with sensitivity to someone else. It means feeling what they are feeling out of a strong sense of solidarity. "We go out from ourselves, we stand alongside the other, we try to share his feelings and aspirations."[4] Compassionate thinking is thinking with compassion about a particular person, or a particular event, or a particular set of circumstances. Someone tells you about a difficulty they are going through, perhaps a loved one

3. John Macquarrie, *Paths in Spirituality*, 26.
4. Ibid.

is terminally ill, or a marriage has broken down, or a child has gotten into the typical difficulties and challenges of adolescence. Do we not talk about our heart "going out" to such people and their concerns? That is compassionate thinking. People may have stopped praying in any formal sense of the word, but it is difficult to believe that most human beings do not experience compassionate thinking in some degree or other. Compassionate thinking is knit into the very fabric of what it means to be a human being.

Then there is a kind of thinking that is responsible thinking. This is thinking that requires some kind of practical response from us. Responsibility is answerability. Responsible thinking makes a claim upon us, a claim that we feel we need to respond to, a demand made upon our persons. Responsible thinking issues in practical action on our part. Responsible thinking is *doing* something. People may have stopped praying formally, but it is very difficult to think of anyone who does not experience responsible thinking in one way or another. Responsible thinking seems to kick in especially in the face of some crisis or emergency—local, national or global. People step up to the plate and respond to the need.

Finally, there is a kind of thinking that we might describe as thankful thinking. This is thinking marked by a strong sense of gratitude. It may be gratitude as a result of a positive health outcome, it may be a thankful sense of well-being in general, perhaps as a result of looking at a beautiful sunset, being in a particularly lovely location. The place elicits or evokes from you the thought and the words, "Thank you," perhaps addressed to no one in particular. You just have to do it. You feel the compulsion to be grateful, having to say "Thank you." Here too people may have stopped praying formally, but it is very difficult to think of someone who never experiences thankful thinking. Even when people do not actually say the words, "Thank you," they often feel thankful. You can see it on people's faces.

Anonymous Praying?

So, there are four basic kinds of thinking that go beyond routine and mechanical thinking: passionate thinking, compassionate thinking, responsible thinking, and thankful thinking. Needless to say, not only Christians engage in these kinds of thinking. Are people praying when they think passionately, compassionately, responsibly and thankfully?

It would be arrogant to suggest that when people are thinking in these ways, even when they have no intention to pray, they are in fact praying. That would be a complete disregard of the integrity of such people. And yet, even if people are unaware of God when they think passionately, compassionately, responsibly and thankfully, they are engaged in what we might call from a Christian point of view "anonymous praying." There is a fundamental acknowledgement on their part through their thinking of something more than the isolated ego. These four kinds of thinking seem to take the person out from the imprisoned confines of the ego to recognize and to acknowledge something more. What is that "something more"? A Christian would argue that that "something more" is the reality of God. Thinking in these four ways is acknowledging the reality of God, even if God is not formally named as such. In other words, God may be known without being named. John Macquarrie, makes the following point: "Prayer is a fundamental style of thinking, passionate and compassionate, responsible and thankful, that is deeply rooted in our humanity and that manifests itself not only among believers but also among serious minded people who do not profess any religious faith. Yet it seems to me that if we follow out the instinct to pray that is in all of us, it will finally bring us to faith in God."[5] It seems to me somewhat too optimistic that this instinct to pray will finally bring people to faith in God, at least if faith is understood here to be explicit faith in God. That does not always happen. Life experiences and environmental circumstances of different kinds can get in the way of explicit faith in God. It is not inevitable that passionate, compassionate, responsible and thankful thinking will end up in conscious relationship with God but it certainly becomes more likely. That may be what Macquarrie is getting at. To think in these ways is anonymously to think about God and his ways with humankind. At the very least, thinking like this is very close to prayer.

Prayer as Thinking and A.C.T.S.

The four ways of thinking—passionate, compassionate, responsible, and thankful—really are the correlate of the four traditional modes of Christian prayer: adoration, contrition, thanksgiving, and supplication, or A.C.T.S. as they have been described in catechetical texts. Let me show you what I mean.

5. Ibid., 30.

If passionate thinking moves me out of the immediacy of self concern, if it moves me out of the routine of the ordinary trivial daily round of living and thinking, this is close to what we have traditionally called adoration. Adoration for Christians is sheer awareness of God, an awareness that trans-figures and trans-forms. We could say that it is a passionate awareness. "Adoration" comes from two Latin words that imply movement out of oneself: *ad*, meaning "towards," and *orare*, meaning "to pray." It is a cumulatively intense awareness of and concentration on God as sheerly present. "The heart of Christian prayer, both for the individual alone and in the gathered community, has always been worship, adoration, the disinterested and preoccupying acknowledgment that at the heart of our reality lies a good and loving and self-dispensing Mystery who is Truth itself."[6] One of my favorite passages in Holy Scripture is that passage attributed to St Paul in the Acts of the Apostles, when St Paul is in Athens, Acts 17:28: "In (God) we live and move and have our being." Reflection on that text tells me that to be is to be "presenced" in God. Adoration is the graceful recognition that it is so, that I am so. Adoration changes a person: "The person who loses himself in the wondering contemplation of God begins to reflect something of the divine glory so that the image of God in which he was made becomes more manifest in his being."[7] Adoration is passionate thinking in a higher key.

Contrition is saying, "I'm sorry," and contrition is another form of passionate thinking. It is taking ownership of our moral failures, our sins before God, not in the direction of excessive guilt and anxiety so much as recognizing that in the enveloping presence of God whose best name is Love, we are so unlovely, and that we have been so unlovely to our sisters and brothers. One author in the tradition of Benedictine spirituality writes: "It is humbling to stand before God with our failures, wounds, chaos, vulnerability. I think we all know deep down that it is only by facing them that we can hope to enlighten the darkness. This means that we must start by grieving honestly and without pretence or excuse."[8] This is passionate thinking in a contrite mode, grieving honestly our sins and

---

6. Brian E. Daley, SJ, "How Should We Pray? Five Guiding Principles," *Crisis* (March, 1994), 29.

7. John Macquarrie, "Adoration," in Gordon S. Wakefield, ed., *A Dictionary of Christian Spirituality* (London: SCM Press, 1983), 308.

8. Esther de Waal, *Lost in Wonder* (Collegeville: The Liturgical Press, 2003), 102.

transgressions, and acknowledging and owning them without pretence or excuse. Contrition is passionate thinking in a higher key also.

Now we move to thanksgiving, the third of the Christian modes of prayer. Thanksgiving is a truly beautiful word. It is surely no coincidence that "Thanksgiving" is the word we use for the central Christian act of prayer and worship, the Eucharist. *Eucharisteo,* in Greek, is " I thank you." To say, "Thank you," is to acknowledge a gift and a gift-giver. "To say thank you for a gift (or as the Greeks would say, to make a eucharist of it) is to recognize it, to think of it, as a communication of love."[9] Thanksgiving is thankful thinking in a higher key.

Finally, there is supplication. This is the mode of prayer in which we ask God on behalf of others or for ourselves. It is a form of prayer that comes with the highest recommendation, that of our blessed Lord Jesus in the Lord's Prayer. The faithful have a very strong, spontaneous sense of praying for one another, and with trust to place all their needs in God's providential hands. At the same time, they have an awareness that requests to God should not be superficially egocentric or obviously trivial. One Catholic scientist, and perhaps one whose prayer patterns have not developed with this basic understanding of life and science, makes this very negative comment about supplication, or petitionary prayer: "For many people, the entire purpose of prayer is to invoke God's intervention in the course of their daily lives, to adjust the tilt of the universe in their personal favor, to redirect the stream of time ever so marginally so that benefices flow their way . . . I struggle to shed the shabby shawl of petitionary and formulaic prayer that I inherited as a child—to reject the default syllables 'Me, Lord, Me'. . . ."[10] While I find myself deeply sympathetic to these sentiments, I also think there is a need to distinguish the shabby shawl of petitionary prayer, the attempt to tilt the universe in our own personal favor, from authentic petitionary prayer which always has the shape of "Thy will be done." It is more a matter of acknowledging: God's holy permeative presence in creation, human interconnectedness or communion, and the mysterious but powerful engagement of both. John Macquarrie puts it like this: "Basically, it seems to me that intercessory prayer provides, as it were,

---

9. Herbert McCabe, OP, *God Still Matters* (New York and London: Continuum, 2002), 68.

10. Chet Raymo, *Climbing Brandon, Science and Faith on Ireland's Holy Mountain* (New York: Walker and Co., 2004), 157, 167.

openings into the dense texture of the human situation through which can come the creative and healing power of the reality we call God; and because within that human situation our lives are all bound together in a mysterious solidarity, then God's power is able to operate far beyond the particular person who offers the prayer, though through him. Prayer, as petition and intercession, helps to make the human reality porous to the divine reality—the whole human reality, and not only that part of it actively engaged in prayer."[11] This seems to avoid any suggestion of magic or manipulation, and philosophically to be about as far as one can go in terms of an intelligible explanation of petitionary prayer. To ask something from God, to ask a favor of God, really is to enter into the mystery that is God, consciously and with awareness, opening our minds and hearts to the transforming and transfiguring reality of his presence. We lay our needs before this God, who always cares for us, who always loves us, who is never absent from us. That is what is meant by making the human reality porous to the divine reality. We go to the God who loves us, we go with our needs, and we go without manipulation into this Mystery of Love. To ask God for anything is ultimately to ask God for himself. God is the ultimate, loving Satisfaction of all our desires, and of all our needs. A mature Christian faith leaves it at that, not only hoping for wonderful things, but *knowing that wonderful things will happen.* The most wonderful thing that will happen is movement, through death, into full communion with this Mystery of Love. There is no other context for the prayer of petition.

The late fourteenth and early fifteenth century mystic, Julian of Norwich, has said it so well: "All shall be well, all shall be well, all manner of things shall be well." That can be the only Christian attitude when asking God for things, the expectation and the anticipation that all shall be well because all shall be well in and with and through God. Julian also writes this: acknowledging all the difficulties that cross our paths in this life, she professes her unwavering confidence in God: "The remedy is that our Lord is with us, protecting us and leading us into the fullness of joy; for our Lord intends this to be an endless joy, that he who will be our bliss when we are there is our protector whilst we are here, our way and our heaven in true love and faithful trust."[12] Julian knows how to ask

---

11. John Macquarrie, *Paths in Spirituality*, 27–28.

12. Julian of Norwich, *Showings*, ed., Edmund Colledge, OSA and James Walsh, SJ (New York-Mahwah, NJ: Paulist Press, 1978), 331.

God for things, and she knows just as well that God is the final Joy in drawing us to himself, growing us to the Bliss that he is, and this is the necessary backdrop to every petition. Every petition, if you like, rendering us porous to the God in whom we live, is essentially a petition for the fullness of joy that God is. Therefore, all is well that ends well, and it shall end well. Supplication, or petitionary prayer, or intercession are all forms of responsible thinking, responsible acting, in a higher key. What petition adds to responsible thinking is an acknowledgement of being in God, of living and moving in God, and of fundamentally knowing that all shall be well.

The Benefits of Prayer

There are very definite practical benefits to prayer. Prayer promotes a sense of unity or wholeness in life. In the course of a day we do so many different things: getting up, grooming and dressing ourselves, preparing food, going to work, becoming engaged in different tasks, and so on and so forth. You could say we live very dispersed lives. Our energies are scattered over so many different things. In fact, sometimes the busy-ness of the day can seem like one thing after another after another. There can be a lack of unity, a lack of wholeness to the day and perhaps to our lives. Our lives can seem altogether broken up, sometimes completely fragmented, leading to a sense of drift, with no integration and no direction. Prayer can be enormously helpful here. Prayer can bring a unity and a wholeness into our existence. If prayer is thinking in the ways described earlier, then prayer provides a vision of life and consequently a perspective that helps to experience the unity of all we do.[13] Thus far, I have been speaking of prayer as thinking, and this necessarily means the use of words. There is another kind of prayer, however, often referred to as contemplation, and this is not necessarily expressed in words.

Contemplation

The Methodist spiritual writer Neville Ward describes contemplation as follows: "In its Christian use (contemplation) normally denotes the kind of prayer in which the mind does not function discursively but is

---

13. John Macquarrie, *Paths in Spirituality*, 33.

arrested in a simple attention and one-pointedness."[14] When our minds are not functioning discursively, we are not thinking. We are wordless. This can be difficult to imagine since silence is so seldom found, and we are so seldom without words, without music, without sound. But perhaps this analogy might help: two people in love. To begin with they are probably silent in each other's presence, not knowing quite what to say. Then they reach a point of confidence with each other, a certain ease with each other that issues in lots of words. After spending hours together, hours that stretch into months and years, words are not so important. Companionship of this kind is expressed in silence. "It is the silence of the full mind, when all has been spoken and summed up and understood, and a new level of communing has been established."[15] This is like contemplation. It is not empty but full. Yet there is no need for a lot of words, and indeed there may be no need for words at all. It is an experience in which the human mind "overflows with the fullness of divine truth, and we are given a foretaste here and now of the vision of God, the vision that gathers up everything in itself."[16]

Conclusion

Prayer is not something that we humans do in order to make God present to us. God is never absent. It is not something we do to make God aware of us, or to make God aware of our needs. How could God be unaware of us and of our needs? God is never unaware. As one author put it with poetic beauty: "God loves us so much that if anyone of us should cease to exist, God would die of sadness."[17] Of course, God cannot die! But this is a paradoxical form of expression—that God would give up God's existence if any of us should cease to exist! That is the extent of God's love for us. Can you imagine what our human living would be like if we really believed that? Prayer is thinking and living out of that fundamental conviction.

---

14. J. Neville Ward, "Contemplation," in Gordon S. Wakefield, ed., *A Dictionary of Christian Spirituality* (London: SCM Press, 1983), 95.

15. John Macquarrie, *Paths in Spirituality*, 36.

16. Ibid., 37, adapted.

17. The Irish Dominican poet-theologian, Fr. Paul Murray, O.P. The source has been misplaced.

CHAPTER TWO

The Lord's Prayer, Challenge, and Comfort

The Lord's Prayer is a summary of the Gospel.

Tertullian, *On Prayer*, 1.

The problem with the Lord's Prayer is neither its content nor its historicity, but its familiarity. Many congregants don't actually think of the meaning of the words or, if they do, find only comfort rather than a challenge.

Amy-Jill Levine.[1]

Introduction

PRAYER IS THINKING, YES, but many of us have learned particular prayers by heart, most especially the Lord's Prayer. It is probably the one prayer that most Christians know across all the confessional divides. This chapter invites us to reflect in a little more depth about the meaning of this favorite prayer. Our two opening quotations bring into synthesis some reflections on the Lord's Prayer. From Tertullian, the late second and early third century Latin theologian from Carthage, we learn that this beautiful prayer given us by Jesus summarizes his Gospel-message. That is the reason why, before initiation into the Christian community, those who are making their way through the catechumenate are presented with a copy of the Lord's Prayer. It clarifies and crystallizes what it means to become a Christian. A Christian is one privileged to pray

---

1. Levine, *The Misunderstood Jew*, 42.

the Lord's Prayer. However, a Christian is one who not only says these words, but whose life is a performance of them. The Jewish scholar of the New Testament, Amy-Jill Levine, warns us that the Lord's Prayer is as much a challenge as it is a comfort. It provides a radical challenge to much in our lives, perhaps especially to our western capitalist, free-enterprise way of living. It tells us that we are the keepers of our sisters and brothers in a fundamental way, and that we may not address God with integrity as Father unless we relate to all others as siblings. Before we embark on the challenges of the Lord's Prayer, however, let us savor first something of its comfort.

The twentieth century Scots poet, Edwin Muir, made the following statement in his autobiography: "Last night, going to bed alone, I suddenly found myself . . . reciting the Lord's Prayer, in a loud, emphatic voice—a thing I had not done for many years—with deep urgency and profound and disturbed emotion. While I went on I grew more composed; as if it had been empty and craving and were being replenished, my soul grew still; every word had a strange fullness of meaning which astonished and delighted me. It was late; I had sat up reading; I was sleepy; but as I stood in the middle of the floor half undressed saying the prayer over and over, meaning after meaning sprang from it; overcoming me again with joyful surprise; and I realized that simple petition was always universal and always inexhaustible, and day by day sanctified human life."[2] Repetition of the Lord's Prayer, learned as a child but left un-prayed for many long years, meant a great deal to Muir on this particular night, so that layer after layer of meaning flowed from that contemplative repetition. The prayer spoke with revelatory power, we might say, to his circumstances. What were the circumstances of this epiphany moment for the poet? Anglican Bishop Kenneth Stevenson helps us understand: "Those words were written by the poet Edwin Muir in his personal diary on the first day of March 1939. He had reached a point of crisis in his life—his wife had been seriously ill, and the storm clouds of European war were looming. Under pressure . . . he found himself returning to a form of words he had learnt as a boy . . ."[3] Global and personal crisis led Edwin Muir to this moment of deep appreciation of the Lord's Prayer because, as the citation from Tertullian at the beginning of the chapter indicates, this

2. Muir, *An Autobiography*, 246.
3. Stevenson, *Abba Father*, 21.

prayer is an intense summary of the Gospel of Jesus—God is Father; the kingdom of God is here and now, and in its fullness still to come; the daily bread of Eucharist is the heart of life; forgiveness of others and of self; staying faithful during times of trial. Jesus lived this prayer himself throughout his life. Not only did Jesus give this prayer to us, but in the giving we are also invited to a gracious submission to his entire message, indeed to the performance of life as he performed it.

When we enquire into the New Testament, however, we find two versions of the Lord's Prayer and, given the contemporary interest in the historical Jesus in our culture, we might find ourselves wondering which version is the more original. So, let us move on to consider the text of the prayer.

The Text of the Lord's Prayer

The two versions of the Lord's Prayer in the New Testament are found in Matthew 6:9–15 and Luke 11:2–4.

Matthew

Our Father who art in heaven,
Hallowed be thy name.
Thy kingdom come,
Thy will be done,
on earth as it is in heaven.
Give us this day our daily bread;
And forgive us our debts,
as we also have forgiven our debtors.
And lead us not into temptation.
but deliver us from evil.

Luke

Father,
Hallowed be thy name.
Thy kingdom come.
Give us each day our daily bread.
And forgive us our trespasses,
For we ourselves forgive

> Everyone who trespasses against us.
> And lead us not into temptation.

The scholarly community tells us that we have here two early Christian catecheses on prayer: in Matthew a Jewish-Christian catechesis on prayer, and in Luke a Gentile-Christian catechesis on prayer. The evangelists were using the Lord's Prayer to teach their communities how to pray. There are various points of difference between their versions of the Lord's Prayer, differences reflecting their respective approaches to catechesis about the prayer. This helps us to recognize that the differences between Matthew and Luke are best understood not as the result of the interference or alteration of the evangelists pure and simple, but rather as the versions of the Lord's Prayer used in two quite different churches. Is it possible to get back to the original version as the Lord Jesus would have taught it? This is an area of scholarly debate, and when all is said and done, it is impossible to arrive at an absolutely certain position. Perhaps we may rest content with some words from the New Testament scholar Joachim Jeremias, one of the greatest Christian Aramaists of the twentieth century, who spent much time studying both the prayer and its background. Jeremias concludes: "The result of our investigation is, therefore, that in *length* the shorter text of Luke is to be regarded as original, and in general *wording* the text of Matthew is to be preferred. Furthermore, we have been brought to see that the Greek text is based on an earlier Aramaic one. If the Lucan version is translated back into Aramaic, the result is a two/four-stress rhythm and a rhyme."[4] This is the informed judgment of but one scholar, but it seems to make good sense. It is very unlikely that St. Luke would have abbreviated what he knew were the actual words of the Lord. These words, somewhat like the eucharistic words during the Last Supper, had a sacral quality to them. Given the Jewish background of St. Matthew's Gospel, we need to recognize that a feature of Jewish poetry is parallelism, saying much the same thing in a variety of ways. Thus, St. Matthew probably expanded the Lord's original words with various parallel Jewish expressions. Whatever position one advocates, the prayer is intensely Jewish, in both expression and meaning. "All versions of the prayer fit within a Jewish context," according to the Jewish New Testament scholar, Amy-Jill Levine.[5]

---

4. Jeremias, *New Testament Theology*, 196.
5. Levine, *The Misunderstood Jew*, 42.

Jeremias also draws attention to the rhythm and rhyme that lie behind the prayer when it is translated from New Testament Greek back into Aramaic, Jesus' own language. If it is said slowly and aloud, the rhythm and rhyme may become apparent. This is what it sounds like in Aramaic:

> `Abba
> yitqaddash semak/ tete malkutak
> lahman delimhar/ hab lan yoma den
> usheboq lan hobenan/ kedishebaqnan le hayyabenan
> wela ta'elinnan le nisyon.

The rhythm and rhyme together suggest that the Aramaic speaking Jesus cast the prayer in this poetic way so as to make it easier to remember. It may even be that through the rhythm and the rhyme the Lord intended it to be sung. We know from the *Letter of Pliny* that the earliest Christians were accustomed to singing especially in liturgical prayer. Pliny describes the Christians of his province in Asia Minor as gathering on the first day of the week to sing prayers to Christ as if to a god.[6] Maybe one of these sung prayers was the rhythmic-rhyming Lord's Prayer.

The Challenges of the Lord's Prayer

Our reflections on the Lord's Prayer, drawing out its many challenges, will be culled from a variety of sources, including especially the *Catechism of the Catholic Church* (CCC).[7] This particular section of the *Catechism* was the work of the gifted Dominican theologian, Jean Corbon, and is full of insight.

Father

Here we have the *Abba* of Jesus. Jesus addressed God as *Abba*, the Aramaic word for "father." Jesus addressed God naturally as *Abba*/Father, whereas our address of God as Father stems from our being in-Christ. It is for us a bold address, as Joachim Jeremias puts it: "Boldness to address God as Father comes from the assurance of being a child: children may say *Abba*."[8] The early work of Joachim Jeremias in his famous book *The*

---

6. See Pliny, *Ep.* X.96, cited in Stevenson, *A New Eusebius*, 18–19.
7. *Catechism of the Catholic Church.*
8. Jeremias, *New Testament Theology*, 197.

Prayers of Jesus made popular for a generation the idea that *Abba* was the equivalent in Aramaic to the English "Daddy" as spoken by little children, and that this usage was unique to Jesus.[9] It seems that later in life Jeremias distanced himself from this position, calling it "a piece of inadmissible naiveté."[10] Adult Jews it seems addressed their fathers as *abba*, not only children, so that it means something like "Dear Father." While research may now demonstrate that *Abba* in addressing God was not absolutely unique to Jesus, there can be little doubt from its preservation in various New Testament passages (Rom. 8:15; Gal. 4:6; Mark 14:36) that it was his habitual and characteristic way of addressing God. Amy-Jill Levine, deliberately and rightly attempting to portray the Jewishness of Jesus, writes: "Nor was Jesus the only Jew to address God as *Abba*, although this may have been a hallmark of his preaching."[11] Levine goes on to point out humorously but accurately that "there need not be a spitting contest about who came up with a prayer using the term (Abba) first," and she also surmises that, indeed, the first person Jesus may have heard use the word *Abba* of God may have been his mother, Miriam.[12] We may safely say that we hear in this address Jesus' customary speech to God his Father. In our using this word "Father" in prayer, we find great and powerful consolation, intimacy, a sense of safety, a ground for hope. At the same time, *Abba*/Father also implies profound challenges.

In the *Catechism of the Catholic Church* # 2779 we read: "Before we make our own this first exclamation of the Lord's Prayer, we must humbly cleanse our hearts of certain false images drawn 'from this world' ... The purification of our hearts has to do with paternal or maternal images, stemming from our personal and cultural history, and influencing our relationship with God. God our Father transcends the categories of the created world." God transcends the categories of the created world, but we are unable to speak of God except in those categories. This leads the Benedictine theologian, Jeremy Driscoll, to say: "Of course, God is neither a he nor a she, and no name and no number of rightly balanced feminine and masculine names can in themselves ever express who God is. But we Christians know God and address ourselves to God in the way

---

9. Jeremias, *The Prayers of Jesus*.

10. According to the New Testament scholar, John Ashton, "Abba," in David N. Freedman, ed., *The Anchor Bible Dictionary*, vol. 1 (New York: Doubleday, 1992), 7.

11. Amy-Jill Levine, op. cit., 43.

12. Ibid., 44.

that Jesus taught us."[13] Fr. Driscoll's point is well made and well taken, but, at the same time, it needs to be acknowledged that there are other ways of addressing God in our rich Christian tradition, for example, as Mother. In Western prayers and theology this may be found in St. Anselm of Canterbury and Julian of Norwich, to name but two. When it comes to Christian prayer, therefore, *Abba*/Father language, because of the Lord Jesus, must have a unique, unparalleled and unparallelable, privileged place in our prayer language, even as we acknowledge other ways of addressing God in our Christian tradition. The key issue is this: addressing God in prayer must come from the heart, without any conscious desire to make an ideological point. Liturgy and prayer can never be reduced to ideology. Nevertheless it must be admitted that some people, for all kinds of reasons both theoretical and practical, find it enormously difficult to address God as "Father," and such people ought never to be marginalized or condemned. The church historian and spiritual theologian Roberta Bondi offers this example: "I have a friend my own age who is an incest survivor; I can't imagine that he ever will be able to pray to God as Father, or Mother, either, for that matter, and I feel certain that that is more than fine with God."[14]

Amy-Jill Levine points out a political dimension to calling God Father. She notes that the Caesars of the Roman Empire were called "father," and she cites the Roman historian Dio Cassius in this respect: "The appellation of 'father' perhaps gives (the Roman Emperors), with regard to us all, a certain authority which fathers once had over their children, not, indeed originally for this, but as an honor and an admonition that they should love those being ruled as children and that they in turn should revere them also as fathers."[15] By addressing God as father, and instructing his disciples so to do, Jesus insists that Rome is not the real nor the true father. Only God is Father of all.

Praying to the Father, as expressed in the *Catechism* # 2779, brings us, embodied in Christ through baptism, into conscious relationship with the Father: "When we pray to the Father, we are in communion with him and with his Son, Jesus Christ . . . We can adore the Father because he has caused us to be reborn to his life by adopting us as his children in his only Son: by Baptism he incorporates us into the Body

---

13. Driscoll, *What Happens at Mass*, 112.
14. Bondi, *A Place to Pray*, 17.
15. Cassius, *Roman History* 18.2–3, cited in Levine, *The Misunderstood Jew*, 45.

of his Christ . . ." True knowledge of God is always simultaneously true relationship in and with God.

"Our" Father

The Lord's Prayer, of course, instructs us to pray "*Our* Father," and not "*my* Father." The *Catechism* # 2791 could not be more powerful in its comment: "If we pray the Our Father sincerely, we leave individualism behind . . ." Being a Christian is both a corporate and a personal experience. Our being persons is only possible, both in our origin and in our development, through other persons, so that one person is no person. That is what is underscored by the little word "our." It utterly undermines our Western penchant for individualism, trying to be independent islands on our own. If gender specific language for God offends some people, it may be, according to Stanley Hauerwas and William Willimon, that the real offense lies in this word "our": "Some people are offended that we are taught to address God as Father. The greater offense may be the little word *Our*. In this prayer we are taught to pray, not as individuals, but as the church."[16] The "our" in "Our Father" releases us from the rigid and narrow confines of our own egos. If all that is implicated in "our" were to be heartfelt and habitually practiced, human life as we know it would be utterly transformed. We would recognize the invitation of *Abba* in the context, situation and plight of the other, whoever the other happened to be.

Who art in heaven

The *Catechism* # 2789 has it right: "This biblical expression does not mean a place ('space'), but a way of being; it does not mean that God is distant, but majestic. Our God is not elsewhere . . . 'Heaven' could also be those who bear the image of the heavenly world, and in whom God dwells and tarries." God is closer to us than we are to ourselves. God is the ground, origin and *telos* of all existence, the One in whom we live and move and have our being. We on pilgrimage here and now are in the process of being "heaven-ed," so to speak, and in this blessed communion of the saints we are in equally close proximity to those who have gone before us marked with the sign of peace. Those who are at rest, finalized in God, are by grace as close to us, indeed closer to us

---

16. Willimon and Hauerwas, *Lord, Teach Us*, 25.

than ever they were in this life. This Christian conviction is profoundly consoling. It is also profoundly hopeful, as Jeremy Driscoll remarks: "When we pray this prayer and acknowledge a Father in heaven, we are already there where we are meant to forever be, within Love's eternal flow. Paradoxically, then, in this moment heaven is revealed as interior to us rather than somehow hopelessly beyond us."[17] That phrase—"we are already there where we are meant to forever be"—encapsulates in immediately intelligible terms the "here and now" along with the "not yet" of the Kingdom of God as proclaimed by Jesus.

> *Hallowed be thy name; thy kingdom come;*
> *thy will be done on earth as it is in heaven*

The three "thou" petitions pray for the coming of the hour when God's glory becomes visible (Name) and he enters upon his rule (Kingdom), "Hallowed be thy name; thy kingdom come; thy will be done on earth as it is in heaven." They are *eschatological* prayers, that is to say prayers for the End, the *telos* of all in God. This *telos* begins here and now, today, in you, in me, as we conduct ourselves as kingdom people. "When we say 'Hallowed be thy name,' we ask that it should be hallowed in us, who are in him; but also in others whom God's grace still awaits, that we may obey the precept that obliges us to pray for everyone, even our enemies . . ."[18]

The "kingdom of God" is creation as God wishes it to be, "the whole of human history invaded by the dynamic of Love that God is— Father, Son and Holy Spirit."[19] It reflects Jewish tradition and theology, distinguishing the "world to come," *olam ha-bah,* with this "world here and now," *olam ha-zeh.* The "world to come" is the perfect messianic age. Praying for the kingdom to come, for the *olam ha-bah,* is exactly the same prayer that brings the Bible to a close, "*Maranatha!* Come, Lord Jesus" (Rev. 22:20). The final coming of this kingdom of God is about the new and eschatological Jerusalem coming down from heaven to earth, "God's space and ours are finally married, integrated at last."[20] This final and finalizing advent of the Lord Jesus is the *telos* for which creation awaits. Indeed, since the Lord really advents in the Eucharist,

---

17. Driscoll, *What Happens at Mass*, 114–15.
18. *Catechism* # 2814.
19. Driscoll, *What Happens at Mass*, 116.
20. Wright, *The Lord and His Prayer*, 24.

"The Kingdom of God has been coming since the Last Supper and, in the Eucharist, it is in our midst . . ."[21] The challenge is to let this kingdom come in my midst, in my within, to let myself be eucharistized. The great early Christian theologian, Origen of Alexandria, called Jesus the *autobasileia,* "the kingdom itself." When we pray "Thy kingdom come," we are praying for this transformation of reality, of one-self, into this Kingdom that is Jesus. This demands change in us. One author, using a musical analogy, puts it like this: "Jesus is the musical genius who wrote the greatest oratorio of all time; we are musicians captivated by his composition ourselves, who now perform it before a world full of muzak and cacophony. The kingdom did indeed come with Jesus; but it will fully come when the world is healed, when the whole creation finally joins the song. It must be Jesus' medicine, it must be Jesus' music."[22]

The final "Thou petition"—"Thy will be done on earth as it is in heaven"—is in essence a petition parallel to the two former petitions. We are praying for this harmony of the Jesus' music, the final healing of our scarred world, and in so praying we are before the Father committing ourselves to performing this Jesus' kingdom music with all the excellence we can command. The question to me, then is: Am I joining in the song? Am I playing the Jesus music? Is the Name being hallowed in and by me? Is the Kingdom coming in me? Is the divine will shown in Jesus demonstrable in me?

Give us this day our daily bread.

There is a strong biblical tradition of seeing this coming kingdom, this end-time, under the image of a great banquet to which all are invited. It is wonderfully caught in the prophet Isaiah 25:6–8:

> On this mountain the Lord of hosts will make for all peoples
> A feast of rich food, a feast of well-aged wines.
> And he will destroy on this mountain
> The shroud over all people.
> He will swallow up death for ever.
> He will wipe away the tears from all faces,
> And the disgrace of his people
> He will take away from all the earth.

---

21. *Catechism* # 2814.
22. Wright, *The Lord and His Prayer*, 30.

This is the "bread" for which we are praying. The bread that finally satisfies, God's banquet bread and wine that soothes and finally heals our grieving and broken hearts. What day is "this day"? What does "daily" mean? In harmony with the established eschatological ethos of the Lord's Prayer, this petition too finds its core meaning in praying for the End. Behind the word "daily" lies in the Greek New Testament the word *epiousios*. This is not a classical Greek word and its precise meaning is somewhat controverted. However, there is a good case to be made for understanding *epiousios* with reference to the Eucharist.[23] The bread for Christians is the Bread of the Kingdom, the Bread/Body/Blood which we already have in the Eucharist—"the specifically Christian sense of this fourth petition, concerns the Bread of Life: the Word of God accepted in faith, the Body of Christ received in the Eucharist."[24] "Tomorrow" refers to the great Tomorrow, when God's reign will finally be established, the great Tomorrow of the Parousia when God will be all in all. Tying these meanings together Jeremy Driscoll comments: "It refers more basically to a long everlasting day that knows no setting of the sun, the day and hour of Christ's Resurrection. So in the end we are praying that we may be inside that day and be fed on the Lord's body and blood."[25]

So much for the consolation of the "daily bread." What about its challenge? Consistent with the eschatology of Jesus, here-and-now and not-yet, there is a very strong earthy, incarnational aspect to "bread." Christians praying this radical prayer are drawn ineluctably into practical awareness of those who lack bread now. "The presence of those who hunger because they lack bread opens up another profound meaning of this petition. The drama of hunger in the world calls Christians who pray sincerely to exercise responsibility towards their brethren, both in their personal behavior and in their solidarity with the human family."[26] Christianity is not gnostic but incarnational. Christian eschatology, and thus praying for eschatological bread, is not gnostic but incarnational. There is no flight from the world with its multiple challenges and problems, but rather a commitment to God in and through this world of God's good creation. This leads Hauerwas and Willimon to say: "So as you learn to pray this prayer, note that you necessarily offer your life to others. Put

23. See LaVerdiere, *The Eucharist*, especially 7–10.
24. *Catechism of the Catholic Church*, # 2835.
25. Driscoll, *What Happens at Mass*, 118–19.
26. *Catechism of the Catholic Church*, # 2831.

as offensively as we know how, Christianity is about your money, about economics. Salvation is material. Certainly, spirituality is about material things, but we believe nothing is more 'spiritual' than money. Through learning to pray this prayer we are taught that our money is not 'ours.' Thus we can be asked to share because what we have is shared."[27] Yet again we are summoned in the prayer to practical consequences of our relationality, or better, our communion with one another.

Christianity is about how we share bread, how we share money, how we share ourselves. A daily, almost taken for granted way of sharing self, is through praying for others, and most especially at the hour of eucharistic communion. This strengthens in an altogether mysterious way this real bond of communion we have with one another. Anglican Bishop Tom Wright helps us to be practical about this in a prayerful manner when he writes: "The next time you come to the Eucharist, bring with you, in mind and heart, someone you know, or know of, or have seen on television, who desperately needs God's bread, literally or metaphorically, today. Bring them with you; let them kneel, in your mind's eye, with you at the altar rail, and let them share the bread and wine with you."[28] Eucharistic sharing or inter-communion is not a regular practice for Catholics and for many this is painful. However, here is a form of eucharistic sharing second to none. It is a real and conscious bringing of others, with all their needs, to Holy Communion with ourselves.

Forgive us our trespasses as we forgive those who trespass against us

The *Catechism* is surely entirely accurate when it affirms: "This petition is astonishing . . . the outpouring of mercy cannot penetrate our hearts as long as we have not forgiven those who have trespassed against us. Love, like the Body of Christ, is indivisible."[29] In the same vein, Joachim Jeremias in his great commentary on the Lord's Prayer says: "As Jesus continually stresses, this readiness is the indispensable prior condition for God's forgiveness (Matt. 5:44; 6:14f; Mark 11:25; Luke 6:28). Where the readiness to forgive is lacking, the petition for God's forgiveness becomes a lie."[30] That last sentence is worth lingering over. Essentially, it

---

27. Willimon and Hauerwas, *Lord, Teach Us*, 76.
28. Wright, *The Lord and His Prayer*, 48.
29. *Catechism of the Catholic Church*, # 2838–40.
30. Jeremias, *New Testament Theology*, 201.

comes down to this: If I am not ready to forgive another for some offence against myself, I am in no position to ask forgiveness of God.

And lead us not into temptation

"Testing, temptation and trial marked out (Jesus') entire public life . . . He was faced with what he called Satanic opposition from his own followers, even from his own chosen right-hand man."[31] Finally, there was the testing in the Garden of Gethsemane, the final testing before his death and resurrection. "Temptation" here probably does not mean only everyday temptations—the kind of temptations we all know about in our own daily lives—so much as the great Trial/Temptation at the End. This reflects the understanding of Rev. 3:10, the message to the chuch of Philadelphia: "Because you have kept my word of patient endurance, I will keep you from the hour of trial (in Greek *peirasmos*) which is coming on the whole world, to try those who dwell upon the earth." It refers in terms of apocalyptic literature to the time of final cosmic crisis. We may also think of it with immediate reference to our own lives: "Help us as we muddle our way through our messy lives, and help us to be faithful right to the end." "Lead us not" for us is not causal. It makes no sense to ask God to stop leading us into temptation! It is much better to understand it as "Preserve us from succumbing to the trials that inevitably will come our way and help us to remain faithful all the way through."

But deliver us from evil.

In the *Catechism* # 2851 we read: "In this petition evil is not an abstraction, but refers to a person, Satan, the Evil One . . ." We are asking God to deliver us from the Evil One. God does not need to be asked for this deliverance. Jesus, God Incarnate, *is* the deliverance. The real point of the petition is to remind us of our ever present, permanent dependence upon the reality of Love that God is. The petition also serves to remind us that deliverance from evil includes deliverance from ourselves, from our worst selves. "Evil is real and powerful. It is not only 'out there,' in other people, but it is present and active within each one of us."[32]

---

31. Wright, *The Lord and His Prayer*, 66–67.
32. Ibid., 71.

Conclusion

The central occasion of the Lord's Prayer in our praying, both liturgical and personal, is in the Eucharist. This is where we pray this prayer before coming to Holy Communion. This is true of the entire Catholic tradition, both East and West. Bishop Kenneth Stevenson remarks that "It is easy to see why. It serves as a bridge between the consecration and the reception of the elements. Indeed, one could hardly find a more dramatic position."[33] The entire celebration of the Eucharist has been leading up to this most intimate moment of Holy Communion. Praying the Lord's Prayer deliberately, reflectively, and conscious of its manifold challenges to us is the best preparation for this moment.

In a fine series of reflections on the Lord's Prayer Bishop N. T. Wright makes the following comment: "Our task is to grow up into the Our Father, to dare to impersonate our older brother, seeking daily bread and daily forgiveness as we do so; to wear his clothes, to walk in his shoes, to feast at his table, to weep with him in the garden, to share his suffering, and to know his victory."[34] While I admire and like these words of Bishop Wright, it sounds like impersonation, as it were, and impersonating our older brother Jesus does not sound right to me. It is not so much that we are trying to look at Jesus, and to look at and pray Jesus' prayer, but more that we are trying to submit to the Jesus-life that is within us through baptism, so that the Lord's Prayer comes appropriately and not just easily to our lips. That submission to the Jesus-life is the work of a life-time, the work of conversion. In that life-time's work the Lord's Prayer is both comfort and challenge.

---

33. Stevenson, *Abba Father*, 28.
34. Wright, *The Lord and His Prayer*, 23.

CHAPTER THREE

Psalm 23

It is striking, the hold that this particular psalm has in the popular religion of our culture. Parents whose hold on Christian belief is not too secure may still teach their children the Lord's Prayer and the Twenty-third Psalm as a kind of double summary of the faith.

William L. Holladay.[1]

Psalm 23 mediates the experience of the peaceful abiding in God which is the deep longing within the human heart.

Dennis Sylva.[2]

Psalm 23

1 The Lord is my shepherd, I shall not want.
2 He makes me lie down in green pastures;
  he leads me beside still waters;
3 he restores my soul.
  He leads me in paths of righteousness
  for his name's sake.
4 Even though I walk through the valley,
  of the shadow of death, I fear no evil;
  for thou art with me;

---

1. Holladay, *The Psalms Through Three Thousand Years*, 6.
2. Sylva, *Psalms and the Transformation of Stress*, 82.

> *thy rod and thy staff—*
> *they comfort me.*
> 5 *Thou preparest a table before me*
> *in the presence of my enemies;*
> *thou anointest my head with oil;*
> *my cup overflows.*
> 6 *Surely goodness and mercy*
> *shall follow me*
> *all the days of my life,*
> *and I shall dwell in the house of the Lord*
> *for ever.*

Introductory Comments

ALONG WITH THE LORD'S Prayer, examined in chapter 2, Psalm 23 is probably among the best-known and best-loved prayers of very ordinary Christians. Indeed, they are closely associated, a "double summary of the faith," something noted by Old Testament scholar William L. Holladay in this anecdote: "I have heard a pastor who intended to lead his congregation in the Lord's Prayer begin mistakenly, 'The Lord is my shepherd.'"[3] Psalm 23 is one of the most beautiful prayers in the Bible, and undoubtedly one put to music more than any other. This leads Walter Brueggemann to say that "It is almost pretentious to comment on this psalm."[4] That is self-evidently so, but it is nevertheless useful to create something of a context for praying this psalm. What can we say about it by way of introduction? The Psalms are notoriously difficult to date with accuracy, but some suggest that this particular psalm may go back to the time of King David who was a shepherd himself and be dated, therefore, to perhaps as early as the tenth century BCE.

Notice the movement of the Psalm. In the first four verses God is imaged as a shepherd (vv. 1–4). In the last two verses God is imaged as the host of a banquet (vv. 5–6). Two quite contrasting images of God! But the movement in the psalm is not only in terms of images of the divine, it is also in terms of the psalmist's thinking. He begins to talk *about* God in vv. 1–3, but quickly that gives way to talk *to* God in vv. 4–6. The psalmist moves from theology to prayer, and of course, as Scripture

---

3. Holladay, *The Psalms Through Three Thousand Years*, 7.
4. Brueggemann, *The Message of the Psalms*, 154.

scholar John Kselman points out, "The purpose of the theology in Psalm 23 (and of all theology!) is communion with God."[5]

The Psalm in Critical Key

v. 1. *The Lord is my shepherd, I shall not want*

In the ancient Near East, shepherds went in front of their flocks, literally "before" their sheep, leading them to pasture, thus engendering a sense of trust and confidence. Ancient Israel knew that God was their Shepherd. Think of Psalm 80:1: "Give ear, O Shepherd of Israel, thou who leads Joseph like a flock!" Our psalmist personalizes this faith, God is "*my* Shepherd." The psalmist affirms that with God as his shepherd, he will lack nothing.

We are so very familiar with the wording of the psalm that its radical claim here may escape us. To claim that with God as our shepherd we will lack nothing stands in strange contrast with our consumerist times. One author puts its strangeness like this: "In the context of a society and an economic system like ours, driven far more by greed than need, the opening line of Psalm 23 is profoundly radical . . . The sense of 'There is nothing I lack . . . is particularly apt in a culture that teaches us to *want everything*. It is difficult for us even to imagine having only the necessities of life—food, drink, shelter/protection. It is perhaps even more difficult for us to accept the message of the opening line of Psalm 23: *God* is the only necessity of life!"[6] Perhaps in times of real personal crisis we become gracefully aware of God as the only necessity of life, a God inclusive of and not in competition with the other manifold blessings of our lives. To pray this line of the psalm is to invite constant awareness of this God, and not to wait for pressure points to arrive.

God is our Shepherd, leading us to life. This God stands clear opposite personified Death (in Hebrew *Moth*) in Psalm 49:14:

> "Like sheep they are appointed for Sheol;
> Death shall be their shepherd."

Konrad Schaefer, OSB makes an interesting comment on this verse: "Death is inevitable for everybody. Those who thought they needed no

---

5. Kselman, "Praying the Psalms," 17.
6. McCann, *A Theological Introduction to the Book of Psalms*, 128.

divine guide end up with a shepherd whose name is Death, who herds them into Sheol to dwell for ever."[7] The Divine Guide-Shepherd herds us not into the absurdity of Sheol, some flimsy, shadowy post-mortem existence, but, as we shall see, into fullness of life, into communion in the Divine Communion.

> *v. 2. He makes me lie down in green pastures;*
> *he leads me beside still waters*

The shepherd looks after the sheep, providing them with food/ pastures and drink/ water. He is very present to them.

> *v. 3. He restores my soul. He leads me in paths of*
> *righteousness for his name's sake*

"Soul" here is not to be thought of in Aristotelian terms as the form of the body. It is broader, more sensuous in resonance embracing "deeper being, living alertness, blood palpitation, breath, sigh, emotional drive, desire, fragrance."[8] "He restores my soul" means that God refreshes me in every aspect of my human flourishing. As a competent and caring shepherd, God leads the psalmist in right ways. He is constantly guiding through all the paths of life. The "name" in Hebrew theology is evocative of character. God's name is God's own character. He does as he is. He is Caring and Compassion, and so he acts with care and compassion in guiding the psalmist throughout life.

> *v. 4. Even though I walk through the valley of the shadow of death, I fear*
> *no evil; for thou art with me; thy rod and thy staff, they comfort me*

Notice how the psalmist's language changes at this point. He has been engaged in theology, in God-talk, in describing his God. Now he moves to prayer, almost as if description of his God necessitates personal and imitate address. Third-person language is no longer appropriate, only second-person will do, "Thou." One of my favorite Psalms-commentators, Artur Weiser comments: "God had been his guide, his refuge, and his comfort on his arduous pilgrimage, and consequently even that painful recollection is transfigured by his feelings of gratitude for that intimate intercourse with God which allows him to face the future without fear

---

7. Schaefer, *Psalms*, 126.
8. Terrien, *The Psalms*, 239.

and with confident hope, no matter what may be in store for him."[9] "Transfigured," "feelings of gratitude," "intimate intercourse with God," "confident hope"—all these words take us back to chapter one and prayer as thinking.

The psalmist is thinking about God, and that is a form of prayer, but his thoughts compel him to praising acknowledgment, and that is the best form of prayer. Even "the valley of the shadow of death" loses its sting with this God because "Thou art with me," in Hebrew *attah 'immadi*, two words only. The psalmist also plays on words: "evil" = *ra'*, with from v. 1 "my shepherd" = *ro'i*. The similarity in English characters between the two words is obvious: no evil/*ra'* but only my Shepherd/*ro'i*. "Rod" and "staff" represent a double description of the shepherd's crook. "The rod and the staff reassure (the psalmist), for they are primarily defensive tools against jackals and wolves that prowl behind the asperities of the slopes. There might also be a hint of disciplinary situations. The rod and staff occasionally help to keep a sheep from going astray or loitering behind the flock."[10] Whatever way you think of it, the meaning behind v. 4 is an absolute, confidence in God known as "Thou."

> *v.5. Thou preparest a table before me in the presence of my enemies;*
> *thou anointest my head with oil, my cup overflows*

The image of God now changes from shepherd to host at the banquet, so much so really that this becomes the climax of Old Testament references to God as host. Weiser sees here the psalmist thinking back to many liturgical feasts in the Temple: "Had he not actually been the guest of God all his life, and had he not been privileged to receive from his hand blessings in abundance, meat and drink, and joy at many festivals?"[11] His host anoints his head with oil, and his cup is never empty. The joyous feast becomes a primary metaphor for God's loving care of the psalmist.

> *v. 6. Surely goodness and mercy shall follow me all the days of my life;*
> *and I shall dwell in the house of the Lord for ever*

"Goodness and mercy," *tob we chesed*, are simply who God is. These are synonyms for the God who is not only leading the psalmist, but following

---

9. Weiser, *The Psalms*, 229–30.
10. Terrien, *The Psalms*, 240.
11. Weiser, *The Psalms*, 230.

him, surrounding him all the days of his life. In this God, we may say, he lives and moves and has his being. God encircles his being, and so he repeats God's sacred name, Yahweh, at the end of the psalm as he pronounced it at the beginning, v. 1 and v. 6. God is at the beginning and at the end of the psalm, and for the psalmist God is at his beginning and at his end. He will dwell in the *Beth Yahweh*, the "house of the Lord," the Temple in Jerusalem forever. Perhaps this is the psalmist's way of saying that he cannot conceive of life without the intimate worship of God at its center. This seems to be what Artur Weiser is getting at when he says: "He will 'dwell' with God 'to the end of the days' and that not only as his guest, but indeed as a member of his household, that is, in a most intimate and unbroken fellowship with God. The main emphasis of these words does lie on the fact of his external nearness to God in the Temple, but on the spiritual aspect of his communion with God."[12]

This communion with God is "forever." Scholars dispute the meaning of this Hebrew term, given the fact that Israel was late in developing a doctrine of post-mortem life with God in resurrection. But perhaps a cigar is just a good smoke, as it were, and the words should be taken at face value! Certainly, this is the meaning that Terrien gives to it: "This masterpiece, in the final analysis, may well have concluded with the hope of life eternal, not through the static anthropology of the immortality of the soul . . . but on account of a most intimate communion with the eternal Yahweh, a bond that could not be disrupted by bodily disintegration. Like few other prayers of the Psalter . . . Psalm 23 does not require submission to the subjective hermeneutic of a *sensus plenior* but needs to be reappraised on the basis of the semantic evolution of its key words."[13] I think Terrien may well be right. Intimacy with God in personal communion, climactically exemplified in the person of our Lord Jesus Christ, is perhaps the ultimate basis for believing that "death will not wipe out (God's) care for the persons he has created."[14] Nonetheless, I do want to proceed to a *sensus plenior*, a "fuller sense" of the Psalm, as we probe it prayerfully.

---

12. Ibid., 231.

13. Terrien, *The Psalms*, 243. Dahood, *Psalms 1–50*, 145–49, also believes the psalmist is speaking of eternal life, "the eternal bliss of Paradise," though many would question his interpretation of eternal life throughout the Psalter.

14. Macquarrie, *Christian Hope*, 127.

The Psalm in Eucharistic Key

Thinking about the psalm in a fuller Christological and eucharistic key takes us to those gospel passages where Jesus is imaged as a shepherd. The most obvious passage is Luke 15:3–6: "So he told them this parable. 'What man of you, having a hundred sheep, if he has lost one of them, does not leave the ninety-nine in the wilderness, and go after the one which is lost, until he finds it? And when he has found it, he lays it on his shoulders, rejoicing. And when he comes home, he calls together his friends and his neighbors, saying to them, 'Rejoice with me, for I have found my sheep which was lost.'" The shepherd in the parable goes after his one lost sheep, finds it and rejoices, and then invites his friends and neighbors to rejoice with him. Is it too much to think of this rejoicing as a festive meal? We recognize the foolishness of God's loving-kindness in leaving the ninety-nine sheep to seek after the one who was lost. This is in character with the divine Shepherd in Psalm 23, and if that Shepherd then becomes host at the banquet, perhaps the Lucan divine Shepherd's rejoicing is to be imagined at a feast also.

That would certainly be the case if we turn to Mark 6:34: "As he landed he saw a great throng, and he had compassion on them, because they were like sheep without a shepherd; and he began to teach them many things." The divine Shepherd, Jesus, notices that those who are seeking him out are like sheep without a shepherd. As we saw in Psalm 23 the shepherd led the sheep, going out in front of them, and so Jesus sees that these sheep are without a leader and "he began to teach them many things." He spoke to them, he offered his words to them, he was their Liturgy of the Word. As Mark 6 continues, it develops the theme of the Eucharist. In v. 41 we are told that Jesus "took, blessed, broke and gave" the bread to the disciples and the people—the fourfold action of the Eucharist. Having taught the people many things as the Liturgy of the Word, he anticipates, as it were, the Last Supper in giving himself to them in this "Liturgy of the Eucharist."

Finally, there is John 10:1–21, the passage in which Jesus proclaims "I am the good shepherd" (v. 14). "Jesus is the model shepherd because he knows his sheep intimately."[15] His intimate knowledge of his sheep and his loving-kindness for them will lead him to "lay down his life for

---

15. Brown, *The Gospel According to John 1–12*, 396.

the sheep" (v. 11), and to offer his life to them in the eucharistic gift of himself (John 6).

Small wonder then that Christ as the Good Shepherd became one of the earliest images of Christ in the art of the patristic period. Perhaps we could say that the imagery of Psalm 23 hints at this incarnational-eucharistic promise. That hint may lead, by way of this *lectio divina*, to a liturgical reading of the "still waters" and "anointing my head with oil." The waters become the waters of baptism, and the anointing becomes the anointing with chrism, and both precede the table and the overflowing cup of the Eucharist. In Eucharistic key, then, water-oil-banquet-table enter us into the bliss of Paradise, into communion in the Communion that is God. This is a psalm to be prayed every day.

CHAPTER FOUR

Praying the Rosary

At its simplest and most obvious, the figure of the Madonna cradling her child on her breast has placed at the center of our experience of the grace of God an unforgettable image of human tenderness and nurture. In its light, the cross is more readily understood as an act of love.

Eamon Duffy[1]

When our brief candle is wasted and this body is laid to final rest, someone may very carefully wrap a rosary around our hands. It is our proper rest. Only thus can we slip decently into the next life. Only thus are we ready to meet our Maker. Whether or not we ever prayed the Rosary during our life, whether the Rosary ever nestled gently in our hands, often our relatives and friends would not consider it fitting to bury us in any other way.

Warren Dicharry, C.M.[2]

Mary and Devotion

FOR COUNTLESS CATHOLICS, LIVING and dead, daily praying has taken the familiar shape of the rosary, nicely and sensitively described above by the late Warren Dicharry in relation to Catholic funerals. The period 1830–1960 was one of intense Mariological discussion and fervent Marian devotion. Think of the devotion to our Lady Mary around

1. Duffy, *Faith of Our Fathers*, 29.
2. Dicharry, *Praying the Rosary*, vii.

the shrines of Lourdes in France and Fatima in Portugal, to mention only two places of pilgrimage. Yet, the two decades following Vatican II (1962–1965) saw a decline in Marian theology and devotion in northern Europe and North America, something noted by the church historian Eamon Duffy: "One of the most striking developments in post-conciliar Catholicism has been the way in which Marian piety simply ceased to feature as a vital dimension of their faith for a growing number of people."[3] Duffy goes on to say that some of this is explicable in terms of the culture of the church. Behind some of the Marian piety of the early and mid-twentieth-century was a sense of alienation, "a sense that in the modern world the Christian had no role except that of denunciation." It is part of the church *against* the world mentality, and so Duffy concludes:

> I have no doubt that (sometimes subliminal) discomfort with such attitudes is partly responsible for the widespread loss of confidence in traditional Mariology, and that any new healthy Marian piety will need to re-orientate itself in order to free itself from this particular cultural, political and psychological heritage . . . Thus Mary's excellences and privileges, like her assumption into heaven, were not alienating measures of her distance from us, but pledges of the dignity which awaits us all, and which, in grace, is already taking shape within us.[4]

Then there was a book published in 2004 by Charlene Spretnak called *Missing Mary*. There are many fine things in this book, some of which would coincide with Duffy's point of view although without his subtle nuances, but central to the book is her very real missing Mary, her sense that something has been missing with regard to devotion to our Lady since Vatican II.[5] Charlene Spretnak is right, up to a point. Devotion to Mary is not quite the same as it was before the Council. Something is missing. Yet in some ways this need not be a matter of great concern. John Henry Newman said it takes a century to receive an ecumenical Council, and in the interim there is the ebb and flow of different positions. Our prayers and devotions develop and change according to circumstances and culture, and in some respects this is what is happening with our Lady and Marian devotion.

3. Eamon Duffy, *Faith of Our Fathers*, 29.
4. Ibid., 34–35.
5. Spretnak, *Missing Mary*.

It is my profound conviction that Marian devotion will not simply disappear. Is this just whistling in the dark? I do not think so. Consider, for example, this persuasive passage from Andrew Greeley, the priest-storyteller-sociologist:

> Catholics live in an enchanted world, a world of statues and holy water, stained-glass and votive candles, saints and religious medals, rosary beads and holy pictures. But these Catholic paraphernalia are mere hints of a deeper and more pervasive religious sensibility which inclines Catholics to see the Holy lurking in creation. As Catholics, we find our houses and our world haunted by a sense that the objects, events, and persons of daily life are revelations of grace.

This is the Catholic sacramental imagination, or more technically analogical imagination. It will not go away, but it will develop. Greeley puts it superbly and with a sense of humor when he writes:

> If the high tradition is to be found in theology books and the documents of the councils, and the papacy, and various hierarchies of the world, the popular tradition is to be found in the rituals, the art, the music, the architecture, the devotions, the stories of ordinary people. If the former can be stated concisely at any given time in creeds which are collections of prose propositions, the latter is fluidly, amorphously, and elusively expressed in stories. Prosaic people that we are, we members of the Catholic elite are inclined to believe that the real Catholicism is that of the high tradition. Doctrine and dogma are more important than experience and narrative... The Christmas crib is popular Catholicism; the decrees of Chalcedon are high Catholicism. The same story of God among us is told by both, the same fundamental reality of our faith is disclosed by both, the same rumor of angels is heard in both. Which, however, has more impact on the lives of ordinary Catholics? Anyone who thinks homoousios is more important to ordinary folk than the Madonna and her Child is incurably prosaic—besides being wrong![6]

As a theologian who writes prose and runs the risk of being prosaic, I cannot go all the way with Greeley. Both the high tradition and the popular tradition are equally important. Indeed, it may even be that they act as mutual correctives to one another. Greeley, however, is surely right

---

6. Greeley, *The Catholic Imagination*, 1, 77–78.

in implying that if the Christmas crib represents popular Christology, the rosary represents popular Mariology.

The Rosary and the Catholic Imagination

Add to Greeley's perspective the following comment from a philosopher: "Icons are filled with the reality to which they refer because the reality expresses itself in the icon. Anybody kissing an icon touches Christ and, kissing, receives his grace. Children already know this when they will not sleep without their comfort blanket."[7] Kissing an icon is touching Christ and his grace. Praying one's rosary is touching Mary, who is most profoundly and uniquely in touch with Christ and his grace. This makes so much sense to me. Catholicism is known as the Christian tradition which is multisensory in its expression and in its experience of God. Catholics like smells and bells! We use incense, we use bells, our olfactory sense and our auditory sense. We use holy pictures, we use bright colors, we use art, our visual sense. We like to touch holy things, like statues, like rosary beads—and so our tactile sense is in touch with the experience of God.

Some people might take issue with the philosopher's likening of icons, and for us rosary beads, with a comfort blanket. I do not think this necessarily takes us to the psychoanalyst for therapy. It's just nice to *feel* the divine, to be "in touch" with God. Matter mediates God and the things of God for Catholics. I like to sleep with my rosary beads under my pillow. What is it about the telling of beads with one's fingers as one prays the rosary? I think part of the answer lies in this need to touch God as it were, to touch our Lady. We have an instinctive human need to reach out and actually touch the divine. Maybe a couple of examples will help. There is a large statue of St Peter in St Peter's Basilica in Rome, and the feet are worn down by pilgrims over many centuries touching and kissing the feet of the statue. This is an expression of the need to touch God, to touch the things of God. Take another example, that of icons. Typically in the West we think of icons as windows into the divine, windows if you will into the heart of God, into the heart of heaven. This seems to be how Orthodox Christians experience icons. Orthodox Christians love to touch the icons, to kiss the icons, and I

---

7. Moyaert, "In Defence of Praying with Images," 612. I owe this reference to my philosopher-son, Dr. Andrew Cummings.

imagine this touching and kissing of icons brings them to an awareness, a tactile awareness of the holy presence of God.

The Rosary Is Theocentric and Christocentric

The very shape of the prayers in the rosary, although it is a Marian devotion, is God centered. Think of how we say the prayers: the Lord's Prayer, the Hail Mary, and the Gloria. The Lord's Prayer is given to us by the Lord Jesus, God in the flesh. We address God in the words he gave to us, the words explored in chapter two above. Then the Hail Mary. The first part of the Hail Mary of course is just the words of Holy Scripture in the Gospel of St Luke, chapters 1–2. The second part of the Hail Mary comes from a Dominican in the fifteenth century. "In the fifteenth century . . . Peter Nigri (d. 1483), composed the second half of the Ave prayer. This addition to the Scriptural words addressed to Mary naturally assumed that Mary has an active role interceding for the church militant and its people. It encouraged having recourse to Mary as an ally in the invocation of Christ and of God."[8] Then, having acknowledged the place of Mary in the history of salvation, having acknowledged her place as first in the communion of the saints, we return with the Gloria to the God with whom we began, only this time in an expressly Trinitarian fashion. So, those who think that this prayer of the Rosary is exclusively Marian could not be further from the truth. This same point is made very well by Pope John Paul II in his encyclical letter on the rosary:

> The Rosary, though clearly Marian in character, is at heart a Christocentric prayer. In the sobriety of its elements, it has all the depth of the gospel message in its entirety, of which it can be said to be a compendium . . . At the most superficial level, the beads often become a simple counting mechanism to mark the succession of Hail Marys. Yet they can also take on a symbolism which can give added depth to contemplation. Here the first thing to note is the way the beads converge upon the crucifix, which both opens and closes the unfolding sequence of prayer. The life and prayer of believers is centered upon Christ. Everything begins from him, everything leads toward him, everything, through him, in the Holy Spirit, attains to the Father.[9]

---

8. Tavard, *The Thousand Faces of the Virgin Mary*, 94.

9. John Paul II, *Apostolic Letter*, 1, 36. See also the helpful commentary of Peter Casarella, "Contemplating Christ Through the Eyes of Mary," 161–73.

The rosary is both theocentric and christocentric. It should also be noted, moreover, that a growing number of our sisters and brothers in the Reformation tradition are discovering the biblical foundation and orientation of the rosary.

Mary and the Christian Praying the Rosary

Pope John Paul II has written: "It can be said that the Rosary is, in some sense, a prayer-commentary on the final chapter of the Vatican II Constitution *Lumen Gentium*, a chapter which discusses the wondrous presence of the Mother of God in the mystery of Christ and the Church."[10] This, of course, reflects the conciliar approach to our Lady, situating her ecclesiologically. Mary is both Mother of the Church, in the proclamation of Pope Paul VI, and the first in the community of disciples. However, if the rosary and Marian devotion are to be recommended to modern Catholics and indeed other Christians, and if they are to avoid the alienation of which Eamon Duffy spoke, then the ecclesiological situating of Mary must be more practically grounded. The challenge is: How is that to be done?

Perhaps a start can be made with some words of Timothy Radcliffe, OP: "The mysteries of the Rosary have been compared with the *Summa Theologiae* of St. Thomas. They tell, in their own way, of how everything comes from God and everything returns to God."[11] If the mysteries are, therefore, theocentric and christocentric, portraying how everything originates in God and finds its *telos* in God, then, the mysteries tell of how *I* come from God and return to God. The Rosary is the proclamation of the "Good News" in the entire event of Jesus, and equally is the proclamation of "good news" to the individual person, to everyone. What Radcliffe implies in practical terms is this: what is said of Mary may be said appropriately of the church, that is to say, of you and of me. Let us explore this through some of the mysteries. From the joyful mysteries, first, the annunciation of the angel Gabriel to Mary. I teach in a building at Mount Angel Seminary called "Annunciation." You can see how appropriate this is for the business of doing theology, and not only with seminarians. The Angel Gabriel brought the good news by invitation to Mary that she was to become pregnant with God. In

---

10. Ibid., 2.
11. Radcliffe, "The Rosary," in his *Sing a New Song*, 295.

learning theology, and teaching theology, we are about the business of becoming pregnant with God. Think of the poem by the poet Edwin Muir mentioned in chapter two, "The Annunciation." There we read that Gabriel's faces shines into Mary's face "Till heaven in hers and earth in his shine steady there." The angel Gabriel encounters Mary of Nazareth, and each reflects the other's face, until she has accepted the grace-filled reality of the incarnation, and until the angel has acknowledged it. Mary is addressed as *kecharitomene,* "Hail, full of grace!" How? The "Lord is with you." Through the Holy Spirit Mary is to bring forth the Son of God (Luke 1:35). Mary puts herself at God's service, "Behold, I am the handmaid of the Lord; let it be to me according to your word" (Luke 1:38). What is said of Mary in this event is said of us, appropriately and with qualification. *We* are "full of grace," in the sense that the "Lord is with us." Through the Holy Spirit we are brought forth as daughters/sons in the Son. We put ourselves at God's service, "Behold, we are the handmaids of the Lord . . ." Go back to the last two lines of Edwin Muir's poem. They apply also to us: "Till heaven in hers and earth in his shine steady there."

The second of the Joyful Mysteries is the visitation of Mary to Elizabeth. The narrative is patterned after the story in 2 Samuel 6, the story of King David dancing before the Ark of the Covenant. We may see Mary as the new Ark of the Covenant, with John the Baptist "dancing" in Elizabeth's womb. Mary is a believer in Elizabeth's words, "Blessed is she who believed . . ." (Luke 1:45). As Scripture scholar, Elaine Park, has it: "Mary is placed centrally among all those who believe; she presents a model for believers and becomes an image of the church."[12] Then Mary proclaims the Magnificat. *We* are arks of the covenant, bearing the Christ presence within us. We are believers. We proclaim the Magnificat too: "When something is magnified, what is already there becomes more evident; it is enlarged for those who would not otherwise see all the details . . . Mary [and we] magnifies, heightens, amplifies the image of God in such a way that those of us who are nearsighted or myopic can see more clearly who God is and how God acts."[13]

The third joyful mystery is the nativity of Jesus. In St Luke's infancy narrative, Jesus is the Son of David, the Savior, born in Bethlehem, and his birth is announced to the shepherds. In St. Matthew's infancy narrative,

12. Hurd, *A Contemplative Rosary,* 18.
13. Ibid., 19.

Jesus is God-with-us, *Emmanuel*. The third joyful mystery is about God coming to birth in our midst. It is about the incarnation. How we may ask is the incarnation about us? It is put best by Meister Eckhart, the medieval Dominican mystic, who makes the point that there is no point to the incarnation unless Christ is coming to incarnation in us.[14]

The sorrowful mysteries almost need no comment in this regard: the agony in the garden of Gethsemane; the scourging at the pillar; the crowning with thorns; the carrying of the cross; the crucifixion and death of Jesus. Each one of them deals with the pain and suffering of Jesus in the last twenty-four hours of his earthly life. It hardly needs to be pointed out that each one of them speaks to our human predicament also. There are times when we are in agony in our own Gethsemane. There are times when we feel scourged at the pillar of life. There is no one who is not crowned with thorns at some time in life. And carrying the cross? We all have crosses to carry. You do not need to look for a cross to carry; the cross of suffering will find you. And then there is the agony of death. The Irish novelist and writer, Nuala O'Faolain, in her autobiographical memoir, wrote the following about Good Friday, as she wandered into the pro-Cathedral in Dublin:

> (I saw) the purple cloths they cover the images with, during Holy Week, to remind us of Christ's Passion. What about the ordinary passion of people! I thought. Look how much ordinary men and women know about being crucified! No wonder we strain ourselves to believe that there is a God, who loves us.[15]

I find that a very sad comment because that is what Good Friday is about, about the crucifixion of ordinary people. Of course, Good Friday/God's Friday is about the historic crucifixion that happened once upon a time in Jerusalem, demonstrating uniquely the *telos* of God's love. But, since we are conjoined to Christ through baptism, Good Friday is about us conjoined with Christ. The sorrowful mysteries of the rosary are not just about our Lord Jesus Christ on the day he died. They are also about our own sorrowful mysteries. Think of the marvelous words of the sixteenth century mystic, Benedict of Canfield (1563–1610), O.F.M.Cap., in his *Rule of Perfection*, 1609:

---

14. This theme is found throughout Meister Eckhart. See, for example, Sermon 24 in *Meister Eckhart, Selected Writings*, 215–22.

15. O'Faolain, *Are You Somebody?* 98.

> Therefore our own pains—insofar as they are not ours but those of Christ—must be deeply respected. How wonderful! And more: our pains are as much to be revered as those of Jesus Christ in His own passion. For if people correctly adore Him with so much devotion in images on the Good Friday cross, why may we not then revere Him on the living cross that we ourselves are?

If the sorrowful mysteries are all about our Blessed Lord, the glorious mysteries are about the glorification of Jesus, and the glorification of Mary s first in the communion of the saints. They are also about our glorification: the resurrection of Jesus; the ascension of Jesus; the descent of the Holy Spirit at Pentecost; the assumption of Mary into heaven; the coronation of Mary as queen of heaven. Let us take just a few examples from the glorious mysteries to see how they apply to us, and not simply to Jesus and Mary. The resurrection of Jesus is also about our resurrection. He is the first one of many brothers. He is the first-fruits to be raised in the harvest of resurrection. We are the remaining harvest. Quite simply, there is no Christ without us. He wants us, and he wants us to be and to experience his finalization in resurrection. Or, consider the descent of the Holy Spirit at Pentecost. The Spirit did not come once only but the Spirit continues to come. The Spirit will always come. Cardinal Basil Hume, Archbishop of Westminster, used to be fond of saying: "Pentecost is today, and every day. Pentecost is today, and always." This is true not just generically for the whole church, but every day for you and me. When we pray this glorious mystery, we are reminding ourselves that today the Holy Spirit is coming to us. Pentecost is ours, today and every day!

What about the luminous mysteries, the mysteries created by Pope John Paul II? The Luminous Mysteries are, he says "five significant moments—'luminous mysteries'—during this phase of Christ's life."[16] They are: the baptism of Jesus; the self manifestation of Christ at the wedding at Cana; the proclamation of the Kingdom of God; the transfiguration of Jesus; the institution of the Eucharist. You can probably see how this will go. Each one of the mysteries refers to a light filled event in the life of the Lord. Just as equally, each one of the mysteries refers to the light filled reality that God's grace makes of us, and the light filled reality we are destined to become. The baptism of Jesus transforms Jesus from being an unknown nobody, as it were, to being a fearless preacher, one totally committed to the reality of his God, his Abba, his Father. Isn't that

---

16. Pope John Paul II, *Apostolic Letter*, 21.

in a sense what baptism does for us? It transforms us from being unknown nobodies into the Body of Christ. We become the Body of Christ in and through baptism. Just as the baptism of Jesus issued in his public proclamation, so our baptism issues in our public proclamation, our public example of what it means to be the Body of Christ, our particular witness to Christian faith. Next, the institution of the Eucharist. I can think of many ways in which the Eucharist and its institution apply to us. Obviously it was the most central event in the whole life of Jesus, on the night before he died. He gave himself away as our food and drink. One of the ways we can be eucharistic as Jesus is eucharistic is by giving ourselves away, even unto death. For example, living our marriage and our sexuality in the light of the Eucharist. Jesus' entire life, was manifestation of the God who is Love; he is about self-gift, and this is especially true of the Eucharist: "This is my body, this is my blood for you." Timothy Radcliffe makes the connection superbly:

> When Jesus hands over his body to the disciples he is vulnerable. He is in their hands for them to do as they wish. One has already sold him, another will deny him, and most of the rest will run away. The gift of his body discloses that sexuality is inseparable from vulnerability. It embodies a tenderness which means that one may get hurt . . . The Last Supper shows us with extreme realism the perils of giving ourselves to anyone. It is not a romantic tryst in a candlelit trattoria . . . The Last Supper is the story of the risk of giving yourself to others.[17]

The marriage vows are explicitly eucharistic: "This is me for you, to death."

These few examples provide some indication of how praying the rosary not only rehearses the central stories of our redemption, the central stories of Scripture with regard to Jesus and with regard to Mary, but also indicate simultaneously how the mysteries of the rosary are our mysteries too. When we pray them, we are thinking. Praying is thinking! We are thinking not simply about Jesus, we are thinking not simply about Mary, but we are also thinking in a particularly intense way about who we are in Christ, about who we are as Christ's holy body. We are praying our own mysteries.

---

17. Radcliffe, *What Is the Point of Being a Christian?* 96.

The Ecumenical Mary

Pope John Paul II wrote: "If properly revitalized, the Rosary is an aid and certainly not a hindrance to ecumenism!"[18] Many Christians who are not Roman Catholic are rediscovering Mary in their own way. Let me draw attention to only one example, Frances M. Young. Professor Frances M. Young is an ordained Methodist minister and theologian. Her area of expertise is patristic theology. Frances is also the mother of Arthur, a severely handicapped man both physically and mentally. She is now retired, and continues (along with Bob, her husband) to care for her son. As a Methodist from the north of Ireland, Frances was not given to devotion to Mary. Mary was clearly a boundary marking serious differences between Catholics and Protestants. However, Frances tells how she was converted to a love of Mary.

There are two moments to her conversion. The first moment had to do with going to a carol service in a local Catholic convent around Christmas time. She took Arthur, her brain-damaged son with her. This is how she describes the situation:

> My hold on faith was tenuous, despite my outward persona as theologian. The severe disabilities of my first-born had been the last straw—the camel often staggered under the weight of doubt and despair. Mostly my soul wandered in a godless wilderness. During the service I was deeply aware of two things: the statue of Mary which dominated the chapel, something I was not used to, and Arthur, in his wheelchair and all too evident since it is impossible to keep him quiet.

As she walked home she composed a joyful poem and in the poem you can feel Frances drawing closer to our Blessed Lady in and through the pain of her son, and also our Blessed Lady drawing closer to Frances in and through the pain of her son. The second moment in Frances's conversion was when she visited Lourdes with Arthur. She was invited to this shrine of Mary by Jean Vanier, the founder of the L'Arche communities. This is what she has to say about the occasion:

> I accepted the invitation with many misgivings—I feared Lourdes would raise all my liberal Protestant hackles. But I found that the place was about purification, not so much miraculous cures as deeper levels of healing and acceptance. Traffic gave way to

---

18. Pope John Paul II, *Apostolic Letter*, 4.

wheelchairs, and the strong received ministry from the weak. In that context I found myself travelling through the passion with Mary, and preaching at her feet on Easter morning at the Anglican Eucharist in the upper basilica. That Easter it became profoundly important to me that she was the vehicle of purification and blessing through her Son.[19]

I have shared this story because I think that Mary is important for all Christians and not just for Catholics. Praying the rosary may be a way of helping to draw all Christians closer to Christ, to Mary, and to one another. Praying the rosary is undoubtedly a classic devotion drawing us closer to the heart of God. Let us conclude with the thoughts of Pope John Paul II:

> Confidently take up the rosary once again. Rediscover the rosary in the light of Scripture, in harmony with the liturgy and in the context of your daily lives . . . The mysteries of the rosary easily draw the mind to a more expansive reflection on the rest of the Gospel, especially when the rosary is prayed in a setting of prolonged recollection.[20]

---

19. Young, "Mary and the Theology of Cyril of Alexandria," 350–51.
20. Pope John Paul II, *Apostolic Letter*, 29, 43.

CHAPTER FIVE

John Henry Newman's *Lead, Kindly Light*

> *I suppose every one has a great deal to say about the Providence of God over him. Every one doubtless is so watched over and tended by Him that at the last day, whether he be saved or not, he will confess that nothing could have been done for him more than had been actually done—and every one will feel his own history as special and singular.*
>
> [John Henry Newman, in his journal for June 25, 1869][1]

Introduction

IF PRAYER IS THINKING, it is necessarily rooted in our experience of life. In some measure, experience of life and our thinking are correlate. The context, the circumstances, the history of our lives, at least, are the how and the why and the that of our thinking. Another way of putting this fairly self-evident point is that our thinking-prayer emerges out of all that happens. That takes us to an understanding of Providence.

It is a fundamental conviction of Christian faith that God loves every human person. The acknowledgment and discernment of this in the life of the individual is the doctrine of Providence, the doctrine that God is with us through thick and thin, or, as the Rite of Marriage puts it, "for better or worse, for richer or poorer, in sickness and in health," until death brings us to our final homecoming in God. "Providence" is never entirely clear to the person as she makes her way through the

---

1. Tristram, *John Henry Newman*, 268.

immediate intricacies of life. Providence is not helpfully understood as God manipulating the course of events for us from outside, so to speak, but is better thought of as God inviting us to recognize and respond to him as the within of our within. As one author has it, "The ordinary outward event is recognized as providential as the divine presence is perceived within."[2] As we move along in life, it is both healthy and good to look back over the years and "see" the hand of God at work, not as a Divine Puppet's hand but as the hand within us, leading, guiding, nudging, inviting perception of his transforming presence. This is especially so when it comes to looking back over the difficulties and challenges that life ineluctably brings to us.

John Henry Newman's poem of 1833, "The Pillar of the Cloud," is particularly helpful in this regard. When Newman entered into his journal the passage cited at the outset of this chapter, he was sixty-eight years old, and he was looking back over the course of what was often a difficult life. As he looked over his life, he was certain that God was always with him, and in all his writing nowhere does he express the conviction more finely than in this poem, "The Pillar of the Cloud." Before coming to the poem, however, it may be helpful briefly to sketch something of Newman's life context. Let us begin with his family, for that is where everyone necessarily begins.

The Newman Family

The spiritual writer, Esther de Waal, has wisely written: "It is never easy to live with other people; it is much simpler to be a saint alone. In a community or a family, or a parish or a group of friends, it is inevitable that we are going to be hurt time and again by others, sometimes so deeply that the pain retains its power for years afterwards."[3] Everyone can readily identify with this sentiment. The Newman family had its own share of problems and challenges. The father, the elder John Newman, had become bankrupt, something that both shamed Newman and left the family in difficult financial circumstances. John Henry contributed as best he could to the family financially, a role that would continue until his mother died and his sisters married in 1836.[4] For the most part, he

2. Strange, "'A Strange Providence': Newman's Illness in Sicily," 160.
3. de Waal, *Seeking God*, 133.
4. Turner, *John Henry Newman*, 122.

got on well with his sisters—Jemima, Harriet and especially the youngest, Mary—less so with his brothers, Francis and Charles.

John Henry put Francis through Oxford University, so that in 1826 Francis achieved a "double first," and was soon elected to a fellowship at Balliol College. He wrote in his journal at times of being "ill tempered with Francis," and then in 1827, "Frank is off my hands, but the rest are now heavier."[5] Francis Newman traveled a very different path from his better-known brother, going on an ill thought out Christian missionary expedition to the Middle East, and moving later in life into various educational institutions as a teacher. It would be impossible to say that Francis and John Henry were close. Starting in 1823, John began a long running debate with Charles who had become involved in a socialist movement devoted to the political and religious thought of Robert Owen. The Irish Newman biographer, Seán O'Faoláin, describes Charles's situation accurately but with a degree of wry humor: "To his heartriven family (Charles) might just as well have declared himself an atheist, an anarchist, an abortionist, or a Roman Catholic."[6] Faced with such odds, one can understand that this fraternal debate, if that is the right word, between Charles and John continued throughout Charles's life. The youngest sister, Mary, born in 1809, died in early January 1828, a devastating blow for Newman. Though Newman seldom commented in his letters on his father's death, he frequently spoke of Mary's. In February 1829, just over a year after Mary's death, he was still dreaming vividly of her.

Newman's State of Mind

In the light of this brief background sketch we can see clearly what historian Hilary Jenkins was getting at when he writes of Newman at the time of the Mediterranean trip:

> Newman was scarred by his experience of life . . . We can recognize major deprivations, first, he had been deprived of his childhood happiness at Ham when the family suffered from his father's bankruptcy; second he had been brutally deprived through the death of his much loved sister, Mary; third, he had felt deprived of his chosen career at Oriel in the defeat of his tutorial policy,

---

5. Tristram, *John Henry Newman*, 210.
6. O'Faoláin, *Newman's Way*, 85.

> which he bitterly resented... The fact that these sadnesses were borne in a Christian manner and did not embitter him in the conventional sense may be the obverse of a pattern confirming his rejection of life as essentially desolate.[7]

A very bleak description. There seems little doubt that Newman went through a period of desolation at the time of the Mediterranean journey, even if he could not quite put those words on it. He needed rest and recovery from the ordinary trials and tribulations of life. He was as we should say today seriously depressed. He needed a breathing space to find himself and to re-direct the course of his life. The external journey of the voyage might hold out hope for an internal journey of self re-discovery and renewal.

The Mediterranean Journey

On December 8, 1832, Newman left Falmouth in England with his close friend Hurrell Froude and his father Archdeacon Froude, for a journey to the Mediterranean, a journey that was to last some seven months. Hurrell Froude was ill, an illness from which he would never recover, but the medical wisdom of the time suggested a warmer climate. He invited Newman along, as his best friend. It was Newman's first trip outside England. It brought him into very close encounters with Catholicism, eliciting from him both positive and negative thoughts of the church. Louis Bouyer, the French Oratorian, writes so descriptively of Newman's attitude to the mainly Catholic Mediterranean peoples of his tour:

> Revolting filth, beggars pushing their way everywhere, sloth, dishonesty—all these shocked (him) as they were calculated to shock any average Anglo-Saxon tourist. Nevertheless, (he) did not fail to detect innumerable evidences of kindliness and humanity. But the basis of their religion seemed on the whole to be a form of idolatry that had virtually no connection whatever with righteous living.[8]

Newman was conflicted about Catholicism. He appreciated the historic expression of Catholicism throughout his travels in the churches, monasteries, art and so forth, but found the popular religious expression

---

7. Jenkins, "The Meaning of the Lyra Apostolica," 134.
8. Bouyer, *Newman, His Life and Spirituality*, 135.

of the faith repulsive. He thought of Catholic devotions in his typical English way as superstitious. He was scandalized at priests roaring with laughter in confessionals in Naples.

During his months abroad, Newman wrote many letters to his family and friends, letters that are not particularly significant, describing as they do the various places he visited and experiences he had, typical tourist letters. However, he also wrote verse, and the verse is more revealing of the inner journey that Newman was undertaking. There were many such verses that have come to be known collectively as the *Lyra Apostolica*. The English literary critic, Roger Sharrock makes an interesting remark of these Mediterranean poems: "The steady flow of poems on the Mediterranean journey may have been partly due to an effort to relieve the tedium of a long voyage. But once Newman got into the vein there is no doubt that a serious part of his mind became engaged by the contemplation of a distant England under the sway of liberalism..."[9] With more time on his hands than he had ever experienced before, Sharrock implies, Newman turned to writing poetry. The poems provide commentary on how he saw the state of the Church of England now that he was geographically removed. The church, due to forces both within and without, was undergoing a forced process of liberalism, but more of that later when we turn to comment on "The Pillar of the Cloud." At the same time, the poems provide a sort of window into Newman's soul. "The verses . . . are significant in revealing the spiritual purification and development he underwent which gave meaning to the entire journey, ending in a conviction that God had a work for him to do in England."[10]

Both at the actual time and later through a series of recountings of what had occurred, Newman came to understand the fearful experience of the illness that befell him in Sicily and his recovery as a providential sign that he must re-order the course of his life.[11] But that did not happen immediately. On April 9, his companions, the Froudes, left to return to England, but Newman remained behind. He wanted to re-visit Sicily on his own, though his friends had cautioned against it. After a few days in Naples, he sailed for Sicily.

---

9. Sharrock, "Newman's Poetry," 50–51.
10. Blehl, *Pilgrim Journey*, 114.
11. Turner, *John Henry Newman*, 153.

He arrived at Messina on April 21 with his Neapolitan servant Gennaro. On April 30 he experienced a fever, but felt better the next day so that he set off again, arriving at the town of Leonforte on May 3. There he succumbed in all probability to typhoid. The servant accompanying Newman, Gennaro, thought his master was on the verge of death. Confined to bed with the illness, he found himself constantly saying to himself, "I have not sinned against the light." This sinning against the light may have been immediately a self-reflection on not taking the advice of the Froudes about the Sicilian trip. Could it have been more?

Just before leaving Oxford to join the Froudes for the trip, Newman preached a sermon, his ninth University sermon, entitled "Willfulness, the Sin of Saul." It was fresh in his mind. Was Newman willful? He thought of the disrespect he had expressed towards his superior, the Provost Edward Hawkins of Oriel College, with whom he had seriously disagreed over educational and theological matters to the point where Hawkins disallowed him any more students. Newman thought he might have received Holy Communion unworthily because he cherished in his heart a measure of resentment against Hawkins, who effectively had deprived him of his tutorship at Oxford: "At the time I was deeply impressed with a feeling that it was a judgment for profaning the Lord's Supper, in having cherished some resentment against the Provost for putting me out of the Tutorship . . ."[12] Could there have been more?

Feeling somewhat better, he set off with Gennaro from Leonforte, but, after walking about seven miles, he collapsed. Subsequently, Newman was taken to a house and cared for over the next three weeks both by a local medical doctor and Gennaro, with the latter sleeping in the same room as Newman who feared being left alone. As the crisis passed, Newman longed for the light of day, and when it came through the shutters in the room, he responded, "O sweet light, God's best gift . . ."[13] Finally, when the fever was spent, Newman moved on by carriage towards Palermo. He was still very weak and unable to walk on his own and about May 26 or 27 found him "profusely weeping, and only able to say that I could not help thinking God has something for me to do at home."[14] It was time to go home.

12. Henry Tristram, *John Henry Newman*, 122.
13. Vincent F. Blehl, *Pilgrim Journey*, 125.
14. Henry Tristram, *John Henry Newman*, 122.

On June 13, Newman sailed from Palermo on an orange boat bound for Marseilles. The boat found itself in a calm in the Straits of Bonifacio, and it was here at sea on June 16 that Newman wrote his "Pillar of the Cloud." After arriving at Marseilles on June 27, he traveled through France, crossed the English Channel, and arrived back in England on July 8. It is fanciful to delve too deeply into Newman's psychology, but the Newman scholar, Joyce Sugg, in a popular little book, may have captured the heart of the "something more" that ailed him when she says: "He went down even further into his past actions and motives, and saw his own 'utter hollowness.' The fever was not clouding his mind at that moment; indeed, he felt that he was seeing himself more clearly than ever before. He was sorry and ashamed . . ."[15]

"The Pillar of the Cloud"

The title of the poem comes from the Book of Exodus. Hilary Jenkins, echoing the sentiments of the consensus of Newman scholars, says: "It is a peculiarity of Newman's literary genius that he should write such clear poetic prose and be such a bad poet . . . The prose can sing, the choice of words seems to be ordained, but the verse so often falls flat."[16] The one exception Jenkins notes to this judgment of Newman's poetry in the *Lyra Apostolica* is this poem entitled "Pillar of the Cloud," best known in English from its opening line, "Lead Kindly Light." It is Newman's "one immortal song."[17] The poem was so personal to Newman that it seems never to have been sung in the Birmingham Oratory during his lifetime.

> *Lead, kindly Light, amid the encircling gloom*
> *Lead Thou me on!*
> *The night is dark, and I am far from home—*
> *Lead Thou me on!*
> *Keep Thou my feet; I do not ask to see*
> *The distant scene—one step enough for me.*
>
> *I was not ever thus, nor pray'd that Thou*
> *Shouldst lead me on.*
> *I loved to choose and see my path, but now*

---

15. Sugg, *Snapdragon*, 57.
16. Jenkins, "The Meaning of the Lyra Apostolica," 117.
17. Honan, "Newman's Poetry," 92.

> *Lead Thou me on!*
> *I loved the garish day, and spite of fears,*
> *Pride ruled my will; remember not past years.*
>
> *So long Thy power hath blest me, sure it still*
> *Will lead me on,*
> *O'er moor and fen, o'er crag and torrent, till*
> *The night is gone;*
> *And with the morn those angel faces smile*
> *Which I have loved long since, and lost awhile.*
>
> Stanza 1

In this first stanza Newman asks God, the "kindly Light," to lead him on. "Lead Thou me on," occurs three times in the poem. It is a prayer trusting in God's kindly providence, to lead Newman on through the tumult of life. He acknowledges that he is far from home. He looks for small steps forward, "one step enough for me." Home is England, yes, but home is also heaven. Life is like a dark journey, like the journey of the ancient Hebrews from slavery in Egypt to their "homeland" flowing with milk and honey. In the Book of Exodus we read: "The Lord went in front of them in a pillar of cloud by day, to lead them along the way, and in a pillar of fire by night, to give them light, so that they might travel by day and by night" (Ex. 13:21). And so, Joyce Sugg comments: "We are like the Israelites released from Egypt, struggling on through the wilderness towards the Promised Land, weary and homesick, but at peace because God is leading us."[18]

He names the darkness in which he finds himself, "the encircling gloom." This is a complex issue, reflecting Newman's illness and undoubted depression but perhaps also his fear of what he called "Liberalism," "the mechanical, mathematical, ecologically disastrous spirit of a disenchanted new order."[19] This new order, descended from the 1798 French Revolution with its proclamation of "liberté, égalité, fraternité" had disastrous results as far as Newman was concerned. Gloom, as Newman saw it, abounded socially, politically and religiously. Liberalism affected religion and the church. A liberal religious spirit was abroad that had even been willing to concede Catholic Emancipation in 1829! The great educationist, Thomas Arnold, headmaster of Rugby School, had called for a comprehensiveness in religion, a coming together of all the

---

18. Sugg, *Snapdragon*, 61.
19. Jenkins, "The Meaning of the Lyra Apostolica," 126.

denominations, but of course, without Roman Catholics and Quakers. Newman saw this "ecumenical" proposal as monstrous. He was afraid that in this temper the Church of England might very well be disestablished, finally demonstrating the victory of liberal thinking to the detriment of the church and its witness in the nation. Life as he understood and experienced it was gloomy indeed. What was the next step for the church? What was the next step for himself? Newman did not know, but he knew that, as in Exodus, in the "pillar of cloud" and the "pillar of fire" the Lord was going in front of him.

Stanza 2

Having trustingly asked God to lead him on, Newman now confesses his sins. Past years had demonstrated perhaps a degree of complacency with his life, especially his life in the church. Newman was well known. He had cut quite an impressive figure at Oxford. He loved "the garish day." He was proud. The Sicilian illness, however, had laid him low. Newman seems to confess in the words "I was not ever thus" that he was not always able to see God's holy yet mysterious presence in his life, inviting him to flourish through a gentle but confident submission, a submission that in its very submitting is far from passive. Newman was marked by a constant and vivid sense of living in God's presence, but his Sicilian illness brought about a much-deepened awareness of this presence. This is how the Newman scholar, Roderick Strange, puts it: "(Newman's) perilous condition brought about a revelation of divine presence . . . His declining fortunes . . . may all have combined, even in him whose sense of God's presence was so vivid, to dull his awareness of that presence. The illness revived it."[20]

Stanza 3

This last stanza has been described as "magically beautiful."[21] Now, aware of God's providential presence as never before, he moves into the unknown future with confident hope. The "kindly Light" will continue to lead him on. This is realist verse. Newman had traveled on a mule through the mountains of Sicily, a tough and dangerous journey over "moor and fen, crag and torrent." The physical dangers were all too real,

---

20. Roderick Strange, "'A Strange Providence': Newman's Illness in Sicily," 127.
21. Daniel J. Honan, "Newman's Poetry," 92.

not least his illness. But God has been with him, and God will lead him on "till the night is gone." The "night" is the gloom of the first stanza—the circumstantial gloom of the Church of England and his own existential gloom. He is full of hope as he waits for the night to pass and the "morn" to arrive.

The loss in death of his sister Mary had a powerful impact on Newman. They shared a strong and intimate bond in the family. Some weeks after Mary's very sudden death, Newman wrote these words of his experience during a horseback journey, the short ride between Oxford and the village of Cuddesdon, just north of the city. In a letter to his sister Jemima of May 10, 1828, he wrote: "Dear Mary seems embodied in every tree and hid behind every hill. What a veil and curtain this world of sense is! Beautiful, but still a veil!"[22] Louis Bouyer thinks that Mary was in Newman's mind when he penned the last two lines of the poem, that she was the first of "those angel faces, loved long since and lost awhile."[23] It may also be the case that he was thinking too of the home he first remembered, the garden at Ham, "where as a child he thought that angel faces were all around him."[24]

So many others in Victorian England found real solace in this poem, including Queen Victoria herself to whom it was read as she lay dying. It may be, thinks Hilary Jenkins, that the last words she heard on earth were:

> *So long thy power hath blest me, sure it still*
> *Will lead me on.*

Mrs. Tait, wife of the Anglican Bishop of London and later Archbishop of Canterbury, lost five children in death in 1856. Beneath the framed picture of her children were the words:

> *And with the morn those angel faces smile,*
> *That I have loved long since and lost awhile.*[25]

---

22. Cited in Jenkins, "The Meaning of the Lyra Apostolica," 119.
23. Louis Bouyer, *Newman, His Life and Spirituality*, 217.
24. Joyce Sugg, *Snapdragon*, 61.
25. Jenkins, "The Meaning of the Lyra Apostolica," 117–18.

Conclusion

"The Pillar of the Cloud" was set to music thirty-two years after it was written by John B. Dykes (1823–1876). It is simply splendid. Newman in point of fact attributed the popularity of the poem to Dykes's musical rendition. While there is something in that, it nonetheless remains true that the poem captivates because it *is* John Henry Newman. Not only is it Newman, but it is also ourselves, as we allow it to penetrate our thoughts before God, the kindly Light, who is leading us too through life "till the night is gone."

CHAPTER SIX

Spirituality and the Arts

Both cinema and church can be "cathedrals" to tell the sacred tale.

Kieran Scott[1]

THE TERM 'SPIRITUALITY' is capable of various meanings and interpretations. As it is being used here, it refers to the person's relationship with the Triune God and also to the resources, mechanisms and techniques that are used to express, cultivate and develop the relationship: liturgy, Sacred Scripture, devotional classics, works of charity, theology, and the arts. The arts? I expect some would be surprised to find the arts in this list, but the arts are important for the development of one's spirituality, though they are not often recognized as such. Since we live in a universe saturated in the God in whom we live and move and have our being, God speaks in varied ways to us, and these ways include the cathedral of the cinema, the chapels, churches and shrines of the arts.

One can always point to various areas of theology that have not been given due consideration, and in-service courses can help to make up for these deficits. There is, however, one enormous gap in theological courses and it has to do with theology and the arts, or spirituality and the arts. Defensively, the argument might run that given the timeframe, so limited for all of us, the arts are a luxury that can ill be afforded. There is so much to squeeze into theological and spiritual formation. A focus on the arts may seem to some nothing short of frivolous.

---

1. Scott, "Communion in the Dark," 14.

There may be some truth in this, but only a grain. This perspective fails to perceive all that is given in the Incarnation. The Christian doctrine of the Incarnation implies that all creation is God-gifted, is shot through with God's presence, that, in the words of Gerard Manley Hopkins, SJ, "The world is charged with the grandeur of God." One is exposed to only a small fraction of God's grandeur in the normal theological curriculum. If the deficit is to be made good in one's theology—and therefore, also in one's spirituality, since the two are necessarily interrelated—perhaps at this time the initiative needs to be taken by the individual person. This reflection intends to provide a rationale for making good the deficit between theology or spirituality and the arts, and also to imply ways in which the arts may be part of prayer.

There is nothing particularly new in this assertion that the arts are problematic or even nonexistent in the typical theological curriculum. Almost fifty years ago, the Anglican theologian, Howard Root, made the point well: "Theologians cannot direct men's minds to God until they are themselves steeped in God's world and in the imaginative productions of his most sensitive and articulate creatures. That in turn is only another way of saying that the enterprise of theology cannot come to life until it takes to heart the principle of Incarnation."[2] There may be some hyperbole in Root's description of artists as God's "most sensitive and articulate creatures"—a description I should prefer to reserve for saints and mystics—but, given some poetic license, this point is well taken. Root continues: "The church has lived in almost total isolation from the arts. Academic theology has lived on its own fat. The supply of fat is running out."[3] Root's judgment is true not only of academic theology, but also of spirituality and indeed of the art and craft of preaching. This includes listening to preaching as well as preaching itself. It is as true of those who hear the homily as it is of those who preach it. If preaching, or listening to preaching, is fed only by one's study of theology or Scripture, necessary as these are, the supply of homiletic fat will quickly run out. Connection needs to be made with people's lives and experiences, including one's own life and one's own experiences, and the arts can enable such connection.

By the arts in this context is meant sculpture, painting, music, poetry, literature, drama, cinema. The list is not intended to be exhaustive,

2. Root, "Beginning All Over Again," 18.
3. Ibid., 19.

but rather it is intended to signal a broad approach to the arts. Nor is it a matter of somehow passively gazing on or noticing the world of the arts. The arts are self-involving. When an artist finishes a particular work and it leaves her hands, it is not complete. It is incomplete because others have to perform that music, respond to that painting, sculpture, poem or whatever the medium happens to be.

Others have to appropriate it for themselves. The purpose of the artist is to alert us to some aspect of reality, including ourselves, that is unfamiliar or had gone unnoticed in his or her judgment. For example, the sculptor, Naum Gabo, puts it like this: "A work of art, restricted to what the artist has put into it, is only part of itself. It only attains full stature with what people and time make of it."[4] In other words, the artist is a creator of meaning, inviting others to co-create meaning through music, sculpture, painting, and so forth. This creation and evocation of meaning is a real, though indirect, experience of God. It is that because it is an attempt to articulate and express what the human really is, and that is the question of God.

"God" is a religious codeword for meaning in its final gracious ultimacy. Karl Rahner takes this insight even further:

> If and insofar as theology is man's reflexive self-expression about himself in the light of divine revelation, we could propose the thesis that theology cannot be complete until it appropriates (the) arts as an integral moment of theology itself. One could take the position that what comes to expression in a Rembrandt painting or a Bruckner symphony is so inspired and borne by divine revelation, by grace and by God's self-communication, that they communicate something about what the human really is in the eyes of God, which cannot be completely translated into verbal theology.[5]

It is interesting that Rahner chose the phrase "borne by divine revelation" for a Rembrandt painting or a Bruckner symphony. The description coincides with his theology of revelation. Rahner distinguishes between "transcendental" revelation and "categorical" revelation. Categorical revelation is revelation articulated and expressed in the words of the biblical record especially. Transcendental revelation is the unthematized, general presence of God which permeates through our consciousness. Rahner

4. Cited in Robinson, *The Language of Mystery*, 36.
5. Rahner, "Theology and the Arts," 24–25.

seems to be situating the arts within the horizon of transcendental revelation, but almost on the boundary with categorical revelation.[6] In my judgment, this is Rahner's dramatic way of inviting us to see that we are always presenced in God, and the point is both to recognize and to respond to that enveloping presence.

One does not, however, have to be a devotee of Rahner's theological system in order to locate the arts within revelation. All art is about revelation. "All revelation is displacement, and art seeks to break open the totality of our conventional perceptions, to stop us from taking reality for granted, to reawaken the sense of wonder."[7] This is true of the Bible as the primary and privileged and unique record of revelation. As God's Word to us it is intended to displace us in the sense of having our placement in the world and our placing of the world challenged.

To take but one example from the Bible, the parables of Jesus have the effect of directly challenging some of the most cherished presuppositions of life. They challenge our taking life for granted. They also stop us taking reality for granted and awaken our sense of wonder. A sense of wonder is, at least incipiently, a sense of God. It lifts us, or perhaps better, it leads us beyond the ordinary, the surface, the mundane dimension of reality to an awareness of the transcendent. The transcendent is mystery, the Mystery that Christians name "God." In so far as the arts lead us to a sense of God we may rightly describe them as "mystagogic," literally, "leading into the mystery." Human creativity bears within it the seeds of the divine, so to speak, but our very creativity in the arts is itself already a response to the gracious divine initiative in creation.

The English theologian, Aidan Nichols, OP., expresses this idea beautifully when he writes: "The spirit of man expresses its own desire for, and striving towards, its Source, by means of art works, themselves stimulated by the material milieu where the Creator Lord signals to us through all his works of creation."[8] This is grace responding to grace. Putting it more concretely, it is the realization that "Creation is already praising God before we have laid a finger on it."[9] In responding with all his creative and imaginative talents and gifts to the grace that is creation, the artist enables creation to become richer and more meaningful. He is

---

6. See O'Meara, "A History of Grace," 76–91.
7. Gorringe, *Discerning Spirit*, 121.
8. Nichols, "On Baptizing the Visual Arts," 76.
9. Begbie, "The Gospel, the Arts, and Our Culture," 70.

not creating art forms and richness *ex nihilo*, but responding and imaginatively to the prevenient richness and form and grace that is already given in creation.

Let us explore one example, the music of Mozart, using the monograph of Hans Küng as a guide.[10] Küng shows Mozart responding in his creative musical genius to God's grace-filled, good creation. Immediately, one appreciates that he is not out to provide an aesthetic appreciation of Mozart pure and simple. Rather, Küng wants to situate Mozart within the sphere of revelation, to see Mozart as a mystagogue. This is how he describes his own experience of listening to Mozart. "If I tried to surrender completely to Mozart's music, without outside disturbances, alone at home or at a concert, I suddenly feel how far I have got away from being confronted with the body of sound: I hear only the form of the music, music and nothing else. It is the music that completely surrounds me, permeates me and suddenly echoes from within. What has happened? I detect that I am directed completely inwards, with eyes and ears, body and spirit; the self is silent, and all external factors, all encounter, all the split between subject and object, has for a moment been overcome. The music is no longer something over against me, but is what embraces me, penetrates me, delights me from within, completely fulfills me. The statement comes to mind: 'In it we live and move and have our being.'"[11]

This lengthy quotation is quite revealing. Küng describes the music of Mozart as completely surrounding him, permeating him, and echoing from within him. Clearly, he is not merely describing the physical consequences of listening to Mozart. He is affected by the listening, indeed changed by the listening. It completely fulfills him and the final words he uses to articulate the experience are St. Paul's words, spoken on the Areopagus in Athens, in Acts 17:27f: "In (God) we live and move and have our being."

In other words, only language about the divine seems capable of conveying the meaning of the experience of the divine. Nothing else will do. This is the mystagogic or the revelatory quality of Mozart's music for Küng. It leads to the satisfying and fulfilling sense of God's presence and encounter with the God present. This mystagogic quality of Mozart can be replicated with regard to other forms depending on the life, context,

---

10. Küng, *Mozart*.
11. Ibid., 32.

background of the person. Others will find poetry, painting, certain movies initiating a mystagogic sense for them.

What can one do on a practical level to involve the arts in one's theology and one's spirituality? Here are some suggestions. First, explore the arts resources in your own community: museums and art galleries, symphonies and orchestras, drama societies and poetry readings, community art projects. There is often more going on in the arts than one realizes, and if one sees the importance of the arts one should encounter them locally. Second, consider taking a course in art history/appreciation or in some other artistic medium at a local college or university. This enriches our capacity to see and to hear, and so to respond to these high points of God's good creation. Third, make a commitment to reading a poem, to looking carefully at an art print every week. Poetry anthologies and reproductions of the classic artists are available in every library. Four, integrate whatever arts exposure you are developing for yourself into your regular prayer life. Use a poem, the painting, the sculpture, the piece of music, the movie to raise your heart and mind to God. Last Lent, a time that I found to be extremely busy in terms of church and family commitments, I made the commitment to listen for fifteen minutes every day to the music of the great cellist Jacqueline du Pré (1945–1987). I found my mind and heart quite simply raised to God through her music—not every day, but most days.

Of course we may choose not to engage the arts for the purposes of theology spirituality and prayer, but in that case we are the losers, not just individually, but as church. Our Christianity will be less than catholic, that is, universal, in its outlook and something will be lacking in the church's mission. The arts can keep the church, theology and spirituality from becoming too cerebral and too inward looking. Aidan Nichols puts it like this:

> If our Catholicism has become at once too wordy and too fixated on structures, then the theology needs to turn from "problems" to "presence"—for in any case, it is only in virtue of the saving presences, and their pressure on our minds and hearts, that problems in this context can be solved at all. And to mediate the presence of the Holy, the church must regain her role as "iconifier"—a bearer of images and mother of artists.[12]

---

12. Nichols, "On Baptizing the Visual Arts," 83.

CHAPTER SEVEN

The Grace of Graham Greene (1904–1991)

We are, in fact, each of us, intolerably complex: confused, bewildered, bombarded by discordant signals and demands, subject to conflictual desires and motives, unstable moods and fragile loyalties; driven by insecurity and ineffectively smothered fear.

Nicholas Lash[1]

IN THE LAST CHAPTER, albeit too briefly, there was a recognition of the enrichment and expansion that the arts may offer to the theologian, the one who prays. Towards the end of the chapter, I tried to illustrate how this works using the examples of Hans Küng's interpretation of Mozart and my Lenten use of Jacqueline du Pré. Now it is time to turn to another creative medium, the novel, and in particular one novel by Graham Greene.

The opening words at the head of the chapter from English Catholic theologian, Nicholas Lash, ring true and describe well, albeit unintentionally, the entire *oeuvre* of the novelist Graham Greene. What is Lash saying about what it means to be human? Despite what may be, at times, well-founded suspicions, no one really knows the interiority of another. We cannot plumb the depths of another's soul or spirituality without necessarily revealing a great deal about ourselves. Without going into the *minutiae* of hermeneutical theory, it can be said that any reading of anyone's biography or any reading of any text that claims our intellectual

---

1. Lash, "On Learning To Be Wise," 358.

struggle, is self-involving, and is self-revealing, and necessarily so. We do not read with empty heads, nor do we read with empty hearts. Our heads and our hearts, our lives and our experience are, quite simply, full of presuppositions, of interpretations, and of preconceived ideas. University of Chicago philosopher Martha C. Nussbaum has written a most interesting book on this subject entitled *Poetic Justice: The Literary Imagination and Public Life*.[2] Without eschewing for a moment the law, scientific rationality or other forms of public reasoning, Nussbaum considers them not to be enough. We need also to engage our own refusals to see what may be there to be seen, perhaps challenging and enlarging our sense of public discourse and reason. "Our society," Nussbaum writes, "is full of refusals to imagine one another with empathy and compassion, refusals from which none of us is free."[3]

Sometimes one comes across an author who forces us into an evaluation of our presuppositions, interpretations, and preconceptions, an author who compels us to look with empathy and compassion at our refusals to imagine one another with empathy and compassion. One such author is Graham Greene. So skilled was he at making us look carefully at our refusals of imagination that he provokes all manner of responses, some quite negative. For example, a recent commentator, John Gray, writes "that many of Greene's novels can be read as propaganda for a slightly heterodox Catholic view of things, in which even the worst human traits can have value so long as they lead somehow to salvation."[4] Immediately, however, this evaluation invites questions: What constitutes heterodoxy, or orthodoxy? The discrimination between heresy and truth certainly has to do with language and meaning, with propositions and statements, but not entirely. It is indeed possible, for example, for someone to recite the Nicene Creed with conviction about the meaning of the statements found there, but perhaps not to appreciate existentially the awful judgment scene of the Gospel of St. Matthew (25:37–40): "Then the righteous will answer him and say, Lord, when did we see you a stranger and welcome you, or naked and clothe you? When did we see you ill or in prison, and visit you? And the king will say to them in reply, 'Amen, I say to you, whatever you did for one of these least brothers of mine, you did for me.'" While orthodoxy is necessarily connected to

2. Nussbaum, *Poetic Justice*.
3. Ibid., xvii.
4. Gray, "A Touch of Evil: Graham Greene," 37.

doctrinal statements and language, it is no less necessarily connected to a radically compassionate style of human living which recognizes the Lord Jesus in the other. Again, what are the "worst human traits"? We might point to the seven deadly sins as displaying something of these traits, and rightly so. It seems to me, however, that if not the worst of human traits, certainly a divisive human trait is to be so certain and sure about the rectitude of one's positions and ideas that effectively one disconnects and is disconnected from the community of meaning in others. The late British philosopher Sir Isaiah Berlin described Greene as "sinister," a not entirely helpful remark.[5] If I describe someone as sinister, an explanation of that claim will say much about myself, my worldview, my values, and it may be that I am missing something, that something about someone eludes my infallible grasp.

Graham Greene

Some moments of Greene's life will help us place his writing. He was born in 1904 near London. Very unhappy in Berkhamsted School where his father had become headmaster, Greene attempted suicide several times. His parents made what was then "a remarkably pioneering decision," sending him at age fifteen to see a psychoanalyst, Kenneth Richmond, a therapist who encouraged him to write and introduced him to some literary friends, including the poet Walter de la Mare.[6] Richmond's influence was to perdure; Greene kept a dream diary for a long time, and to some extent may be considered a psychological novelist. He moved on to Balliol College, Oxford, in 1922 where, according to himself, he spent most of his time drunk and debt-ridden. But he also gained considerable experience as a writer.

Graduating in 1925, Greene got a job as subeditor with the *Nottingham Journal*, and it was while in Nottingham that he met his future wife, Vivien Dayrell-Browning. She had written to him to correct some misunderstandings about Catholicism in his work. It was her influence that brought him to instruction with Father Trollope at the cathedral in Nottingham and so into the Catholic Church in 1926.

Moving on from Nottingham to London, Greene married Vivien in 1927 and worked for *The Times*. His novel writing began in earnest now

5. Ibid., 38.
6. Miller, *Understanding Graham Greene*, 3.

but did not meet with great success immediately, and it was with some trepidation that he left the financial security of *The Times* to set out as a self-employed writer. In addition to writing novels, he became involved in screen-writing and traveling. His experience of the religious purges of 1938 in Mexico provided the foundations for his novel, *The Power and the Glory* (1940), which many consider his finest novel. It won the Hawthornden Prize in 1941, and condemnation by the Vatican. During World War II, he worked for the British Secret Service, MI6, in Sierra Leone, which became the setting for *The Heart of the Matter* (1948), and it is to this novel that attention will be given.

Financially successful and famous by this time, Greene lived very comfortably in London, Antibes, and Capri. He had many extra-marital affairs and confessed himself to be a bad husband and an unreliable lover. Though he and Vivien separated in 1948, they never divorced. Toward the end of his life, Greene lived in Vevey, Switzerland, along with his companion, Yvonne Cloetta, and he died there on April 3, 1991. His was a very complicated human journey.

Novels are important in theological reflection and spirituality. American theologian Robert P. Scharlemann reflects that just as

> Sacred music can let grace be heard, even when words have become too corroded or distorted to do so, this is parallel to a phenomenon widely recognized today, namely, that many people learn more of the substance of theology indirectly by way of novels than directly by way of theological treatises.[7]

Whatever one thinks of the corrosion or distortion of human words—and there is plenty of direct and personal human evidence of it—people do learn a great deal of theology, consciously or unconsciously through the reading of novels, and indeed, through their portrayal in movies. Greene was both novelist and screen-writer, and he wanted himself to be understood as a novelist who happened to be a Catholic, rather than a Catholic novelist. Whatever this might mean, and it is debated, what cannot be denied is the "iconology of Catholicism" throughout his work.[8] The icons are everywhere, as he shows religion (Catholicism in particular) to be a central influence in the lives of his characters.

---

7. Scharlemann, *Inscriptions and Reflections*, 160.
8. Miller, *Understanding Graham Greene*, 12.

The Heart of the Matter[9]

The Heart of the Matter occupies several months in the life of Major Henry Scobie. Scobie is a complicated man and arguably reflects something of Graham Greene's own complexity. After fifteen years of colonial service in Sierra Leone, Scobie is, for all practical purposes, broken by the circumstances of his life. The Second World War is on, and his posting is in a relatively insignificant British colony. At forty-nine, he is the assistant commissioner of police. His only child is dead, and he is unable to communicate with his wife, Louise, whom he no longer loves. She has become somewhat neurotic after the death of their child, and Scobie feels for her something akin to pity and responsibility. He overhears her referred to as "literary Louise," because of her interest in poetry and literature, and is offended by the remark. An acquaintance says of the Scobies' marriage and in reference to a rumor of the major's infidelity, "Perhaps if I had a wife like that, I'd sleep with niggers too."[10] In actual fact, there is no basis for Scobie's infidelity other than some degree of openness on his part to the natives, an openness not widely shared in colonial circles.

There are additional difficulties. The Scobies have been slighted: Scobie has been passed over for promotion, and Louise is not pleased. Her displeasure has been all too accurately summarized in this way: "In the small, spitefully intimate colonial society, Louise feels the slight keenly, and vents her spleen on the long-suffering Scobie."[11] She would like to go to South Africa for a vacation to get away from it all, but there is a problem with money. Scobie approaches his local bank manager for a loan but is turned down, and this leads him to dealing with a dishonest Syrian trader, Yusef.

At the end of Book One, Scobie has obtained the money he needs from Yusef, and so Louise is off for her vacation. At the beginning of Book Two, Scobie is receiving survivors from a torpedoed ship and visits the hospital where the survivors are recovering. He gives comfort to a dying child in her last moments by making the shadow of a rabbit's head on the wall with his hands; Scobie even prays for the little girl: "Father . . . give her peace. Take away my peace for ever, but give her peace."

---

9. Greene, *The Heart of the Matter*. [Hereafter, *Heart*.]
10. *Heart*, 14.
11. Lodge, *Graham Greene*, 28.

The dying child says, "Father," thinking Scobie to be her dead father. He remains with the child until she dies: "Yes, dear. Don't speak. I'm here."[12] He also meets in the hospital Helen Rolt, a nineteen-year-old woman and now a widow after only one month of marriage—her husband had died in the open boat in which she survived. Scobie helps Helen, who becomes his friend and lover.

After a quarrel with Helen, Scobie writes a letter to her protesting his love for her, but the letter is intercepted by a servant of the unscrupulous Yusef and is used to blackmail Scobie into diamond smuggling. In this never received letter, Scobie wrote, "I love you more than myself, more than my wife, more than God I think."[13] The letter is extraordinarily significant in the novel. One author comments on it as follows: "The letter to Helen is the high water mark of the novel's action . . . It commits him just as inexorably to Helen as he is already to his wife by the marriage bond . . . What began as a vague sense of responsibility is now weighted with a nuance, even a sacramental dignity . . . The rest of the action is but an elaboration of this one tragic decision."[14]

In Book Three, Louise returns from her South African vacation. She is resigned to Scobie's failure to achieve promotion but now sees it as her mission in life to be the custodian of his religious duties and observance. She wants him to receive Holy Communion with her. Scobie, as a Catholic, cannot go to the Sacrament without first receiving forgiveness in the sacrament of confession and penance for his adultery. His confessor, the Catholic priest Father Rank, refuses forgiveness because there is no firm purpose of amendment on Scobie's part because Scobie refuses to give up Helen. He needs, however, to keep up appearances for his own sake, as faithful husband, and as a faithful lover. He approaches the sacrament:

> Father Rank came down the steps from the altar bearing the Host. The saliva had dried in Scobie's mouth: it was as though his veins had dried. He couldn't look up; he saw only the priest's skirt like the skirt of the medieval warhorse bearing down upon him: the flapping of feet: the charge of God. If only the archers would let fly from ambush, and for a moment he dreamed that the priest's steps had indeed faltered: perhaps after all something may yet happen before he reaches me: some incredible interposition . . .

---

12. *Heart*, 125.
13. Ibid., 181.
14. Kurismmootil, *Heaven and Hell on Earth*, 116–17.

> But with open mouth (the time had come) he made one last attempt at prayer, "O God, I offer up my damnation to you. Take it. Use it for them," and was aware of the pale papery taste of an eternal sentence on the tongue.[15]

In his own eyes he was damning himself, but in order to defend the two women he judged to be helpless without him. In a subsequent conversation with Helen, when he tells her that he has condemned himself to Hell in receiving the Eucharist unworthily, she accuses him of having done so not out of love for her but because he was afraid that Louise would find out about their affair. Scobie responds: "'Love for both of you. If it were just for her, there'd be an easy straight way. He put his hands over his eyes, feeling hysteria beginning to mount again. He said, 'I can't bear to see suffering, and I cause it all the time. I want to get out, get out.'"[16]

As if to confirm his own self-condemnation during this moral and spiritual malaise, and as he is about to deliver contraband diamonds, Scobie foolishly distrusts his loyal servant, Ali. In a drunken state he shares with Yusef his doubts about Ali's trustworthiness, doubts utterly without any foundation in fact, and Yusef assures Scobie that he will take care of Ali. This he does by having the man murdered. Scobie finds Ali's body, and he sees it as "like a broken piece of the rosary . . . a couple of black beads and the image of God coiled at the end of it. Oh God, he thought, I've killed you: you've served me all these years and I've killed you at the end of them. God lay there under the petrol drums . . ."[17]

There is no more hope left in Scobie's sad life. For the sake of Louise he plans a suicide that will look like natural death. He pretends to have angina, stockpiles the regular doses of medicine, and prepares to overdose. Shortly before doing so, however, he learns that the job for which he had been passed over will now be his, that is, commissioner of police. After being told that he is the man for the job, Scobie thinks:

> So all this need not have happened. If Louise had stayed, I should never have loved Helen, I would never have been blackmailed by Yusef never committed that act of despair. I would have been myself still . . . But, of course, he told himself it's only because I have done these things that success comes. I am of the devil's

15. *Heart*, 225.
16. Ibid., 233.
17. Ibid.

party. He looks after his own in this world. I shall go now from damned success to damned success, he thought with disgust.[18]

But for Him It Is Now Too, Too Late

After taking the overdose of medication, Greene describes Scobie's last words and his death: "He said aloud, 'Dear God, I love . . .' but the effort was too great and he did not feel his body when it struck the floor or hear the small tinkle of the medal as it span like a coin under the ice-box—the saints whose name nobody could remember."[19] Who is it Scobie loves? "Dear God, I love . . ." One can make a case for Louise, for Helen, for Ali. One can make a case for God. Personally, I think a case can be made for loving the Love that God is, and for others in and through and with that God, not outside God. It may be objected that I am reading Scobie's last words through my own experience, but is there some other, more authentic way?

Louise finally goes to see Father Rank. She needs to speak to him about her husband, his suicide and his adultery. She is hurt and wounded, and in need of deep healing. She tells Rank that Scobie was "a bad Catholic." The priest responds: "That's the silliest phrase in common use."[20] She goes on to say to the priest that there is no point whatsoever in praying for her suicide husband, because suicide puts one beyond the pale of God's mercy and love. Such prayer is an absolute waste of time. Fr. Rank replies: "For goodness' sake, Mrs. Scobie, don't imagine you—or I—know a thing about God's mercy." "The Church says . . . ," she interrupts. "I know the Church says," Rank responds. "The Church knows all the rules. But it doesn't know what goes on in a single human heart."[21]

The Grace of Graham Greene

The contemporary Catholic novelist and literary critic David Lodge makes the following statement about Graham Greene: "Belonging by

---

18. Ibid., 228.
19. Ibid., 265.
20. Ibid., 281.
21. Ibid., 272. See the interesting comments of Ker, "The Catholicism of Greeneland," 142.

language and nationality to a tradition in the novel based essentially on the values of secularized Protestantism, Greene has adopted the alien dogmatic system of Roman Catholicism, and put it at the very center of his mature work."[22] Lodge is undoubtedly correct, but, when it comes to *The Heart of the Matter* and to the person of Scobie, there has emerged among the critics no real consensus about its meaning.[23] To demonstrate this, let me pick up two recent commentators, Lisa Crumley Bierman, a literary critic, and Paul J. Wadell, a theologian.

Lisa Bierman sees Scobie as having "tailored and customized his adopted religion to fit into his own generally skewed version of the world." He has his own invented version of Catholicism."[24] I am curious as to the meaning of the verbs "tailor," "customize" and "invent." Can anyone be entirely free of these actions? As each of us attempts to be faithful to Christ, we incarnate in the precious and fleeting moments of our own lives those aspects of the Christ-vision we judge to be most important. We necessarily tailor, customize, and, to some degree, invent. This attempted, ongoing, daily incarnation is the best that can be done. We struggle to make the Christ-vision our own, and the agony marks the entire course of our lives. Bierman sees Scobie placing himself on the same level as God, and thus removing all possibility of hope for himself, instituting a world that is devoid of compassionate love, peace, and meaning.[25] While she shows real insight in the interplay of characters—Scobie, Louise, Helen—she judges that "the portrait painted of the pitying Scobie is more pathetic than sympathetic."[26] The great strength of Bierman's analysis is to point up our human freedom, and how we are responsible for our actions and for their consequences. No disagreement there. But freedom is always contextualized in this person or that, is always marked by limitations, and carries the impress of a particular culture, family, and personal history. Bierman's interpretation leaves no room for the pervasive ambiguity of human living, and is much too harsh.

---

22. Lodge, *Graham Greene*, 4.

23. Kurismmootil, *Heaven and Hell on Earth*, 122.

24. Bierman, "Scobie Reconsidered," 65. A not dissimilar reading of Greene and of Scobie may be found in the Catholic theologian, Hilda Graef, *Modern Gloom and Christian Hope*, 84–97.

25. Bierman, "Scobie Reconsidered," 68.

26. Ibid., 73.

Theologian Paul Wadell writes of Graham Greene: "Who of us understands our own hearts? Why are we so good at self-sabotage? Why do we consistently fall short of the love and goodness for which we are made? Why do we sometimes stumble more than we soar? Why do we know more scoundrels than saints? . . . [Graham Greene is] a master at depicting the depths of human brokenness and the ease with which we stray."[27] Wadell recognizes our human freedom, and the false choices we make as moral agents. There is no retreat from our sinfulness in his view. But there is room for ambiguity, for fragility, and failure is not necessarily final. Have I set up the contrast between Bierman's and Wadell's readings of Scobie so as to favor Wadell over Bierman? Yes! The reading of a novel, watching a movie, engaging with a poem or a play is a process in which conversation is ongoing. Conversation is courteous but vigorous listening and responding. I leave the conversation of the novel with a definite view, a view that yields what I would call *sanitas*, sanity, health, a sense of wholeness and completeness, and yet a virtual sense of wholeness and completeness, rather than an absolute sense. Virtual because, if I am not open to the self-correcting process of learning that is at the heart of genuine conversation, I am locked into a destructive narcissism.

The journey of Scobie is the journey of everyone. It is true that the journey reveals human pettiness and human sinfulness. There can be no denial of that. But is that sinister, in Isaiah Berlin's words?[28] I don't think so. It seems to be Christian realism and self-knowledge. "All is not well with us. Contradictions flourish in our lives. We are well aware of our patterns of destructiveness, but knowing them does not stop us from embracing them . . . Nothing in us is quite as it should be and we know this every time we hurt the ones we most want to love and every time we allow our best self to be lost."[29] The other side of this coin of Christian recognition of pettiness and sinfulness is this: "a God who is love does not want anyone to be lost."[30] God and, therefore grace, God's presence in our lives, is always ahead of us, more intimate to us than we are to ourselves, and Graham Greene stands for that basic conviction that we cannot eliminate the reality of this gracious God, even when we turn from the light. We may turn from the light but the light never turns from

---

27. Wadell, *The Moral of the Story*, 41.
28. John Gray, "A Touch of Evil: Graham Greene," 37.
29. Paul Wadell, *The Moral of the Story*, 44.
30. Ibid., 42.

us. There is always hope. Wadell concludes: "In the end, Greene insists, everyone is saved not by her or his goodness or virtue, but by a God who never gives up on us and a God whose love refuses to let us be lost."[31]

The grace of Graham Greene lies in recognizing and struggling with the ambiguities not of life in general, but of our own individual lives, even as we strive to remain faithful to God. The grace of Graham Greene lies in accepting our complexity, our fragility, our permeative sense of incompleteness, and yet in not giving up. The grace of Graham Greene lies in glimpsing, albeit occasionally and partially, that our holy God is "the Love that will not let us go."[32] Graham Greene is not the only novelist whose imaginative work may help us to think more carefully about God, and, therefore, to pray. However, he provides us with an example, a novel and a little literary criticism, to demonstrate how the reading of fiction may enlarge our capacity to pray.

---

31. Ibid., 52.
32. *The United Methodist Hymnal*, # 480.

CHAPTER EIGHT

The Eucharist Makes the Church

The Eucharist is the Church

Joseph Ratzinger/Pope Benedict XVI

Now it is time to turn from the prayer life of the individual person on her or his own, to the corporate and liturgical prayer of the Church, and in particular to the Eucharist. The Eucharist makes the Church. This chapter will attempt to exemplify this axiom of Eucharistic theology by setting out on an historical pilgrimage. Pilgrimage is such an appropriate metaphor for the entirety of the Christian life. Pilgrimage reminds us that there is a goal to our human journey, the goal of the kingdom of heaven, the goal of full communion with the Trinity. This is "the goal of the pilgrim in the Christian tradition . . . where he is at home and welcomed. Already in some sense he is at home, in the Eucharistic assembly, which meets *in via* and yet is a genuine experience, in anticipation, of the marriage supper of the Lamb, the feasting in the new Jerusalem."[1]

So, we shall set out on pilgrimage to Corinth in Greece in 56 AD, then to Jerusalem in Palestine about 380 AD. Turning westward, we shall travel to Hippo, North Africa, in the late fourth and early fifth centuries. Antwerp in Flanders and Magdeburg in Germany in the thirteenth century will be our next stop before moving on to Norwich, in the southeast

---

1. Preston, *Faces of the Church*, 224. This chapter in Fr. Preston's beautiful book is entitled "Pilgrims."

of England in the fourteenth century. In these places we shall meet men and women who will offer us a rich sense of the Eucharist making the church.

Paul, Cyril, and Augustine

St. Paul is the earliest Christian author to write about the Eucharist. In his First Letter to the Corinthians, chapter 11, we have the earliest eucharistic text in the Christian tradition, predating the institution narratives of the Gospels by some two decades. In chapter 11, verses 23–26, Paul provides us with the basic narrative of institution, that the Lord, on the night he was handed over, took bread, gave thanks, broke it and said, "This is my body that is for you. Do this in remembrance of me" (v. 24). Likewise, after supper, "This is the new covenant in my blood . . . As often as you eat this bread and drink the cup, you proclaim the death of the Lord until he comes" (v. 26). These words are familiar to us from the celebration of the Eucharist. It is the next three verses that are of interest to us because of the challenge they represent: "Therefore, whoever eats the bread or drinks the cup of the Lord unworthily will have to answer for the body and blood of the Lord (27). A person should examine himself, and so eat the bread and drink the cup (28). For anyone who eats and drinks without discerning the body, eats and drinks judgment on himself (29)." Verse 27 insists that eating and drinking the eucharistic gifts unworthily is a sin against the Lord. And so, verse 28 goes on to say that people should test themselves before eating and drinking. The ultimate test seems to come in verse 30, that a person should "discern the body" so as to avoid eating and drinking judgment on himself. What does Paul mean by "discerning the body"? To answer this question adequately, we need to have some grasp of the problems and difficulties facing the Corinthian Christian community.

There are divisions (Paul's actual word is "schisms") in this community (chapters 1–4). Misuse of the body and questions concerning sexuality and marriage arise (chapters 5–7). A crucial issue seems to have been whether Christians could eat meat that had been sacrificed to idols, and then sold in the market place (chapters 8–9). Use and abuse of the gifts of the Spirit and questions concerning the resurrection are also dividing this community (chapters 12–15). Paul addresses all of these issues, and one of his concerns is to point up the unity that ought to exist among Christians. He maintains that the cup of blessing that they share and the bread that they break forms them into a communion in Christ, a communion with the Lord and a communion with one another. The word Paul uses is a word that has become important in theology and spirituality, the word *koinonia*. The Lord's Supper was celebrated in the context of a common meal in the community, but it appears that some began their meal, perhaps having access to the best food and drink, while caring little for those who came late, perhaps the slaves. "Discerning the body" for Paul seems to mean both being able to discern the eucharistic gifts at the meal, recognizing them as different from whatever food was available, and also discerning the Body of Christ that is the church. It is impossible to discern the eucharistic body without at the same time discerning the ecclesial body for Paul. The one is related to the other. A love of the eucharistic Christ given in bread and cup, demands a love of the ecclesial Christ, given in brother and sister. "To threaten the common union established by the Lord between himself and his community, and within the community itself, by an arrogant exercising of one's privileges, is unacceptable—and dangerous."[2]

Cyril was appointed Bishop of Jerusalem in 350 AD. This was after the peace of Constantine, when the church was no longer subject to persecution by the Roman imperial authorities, and also when it began to witness more ornate liturgies, the catechumenate, and the building of churches. As Bishop of Jerusalem, one of several of Cyril's responsibilities was to prepare people for the sacraments of Christian initiation, and his addresses to the catechumens of Jerusalem have come down to us, "an invaluable liturgical legacy, the earliest complete set of extant baptismal instructions in ancient Christianity."[3] Cyril takes as his point of departure the realism of the words of our Lord at the Last Supper, "Take, eat this is my body . . . Take, drink, this is my blood." The body and blood of Christ are given to us "in the figure" of bread and wine. The word Cyril uses for "figure" is the Greek word *typos*, the closest English equivalent being "sacrament." Type or figure for Cyril means that this *is* Christ's body and blood, though not obviously so. Though he would not have put it like this, Cyril means that the type is the efficacious sacramental sign of Christ. It is truly and really the reality of Christ, or everything else Cyril has to say about this issue is meaningless.

2. Moloney, *A Body Broken for a Broken People*, 117.
3. Finn, *From Death to Rebirth*, 194.

As a result of eating and drinking the body and blood of Christ, Cyril tells us that we become of "the same body and the same blood with him . . . we become partakers of the divine nature."[4] That phrase, "the same body and the same blood with him," in Greek is actually two words, *syssomos* and *synaimos*. In English it takes nine words to translate the idea, but the mere two Greek words are more powerfully suggestive of the dynamic union that occurs between the believer and Christ through the Eucharist. The words say something like "Christ bodies us with himself, bloods us with himself." That sounds cumbersome, but it captures something of the profound union between Christ and the Church. This eucharistic union renders us *koinonoi* with the divine nature, the same words Paul uses in 1 Corinthians 10:16. "Partakers" sounds much too bland to communicate this. Something like "communioned in and with God" is more literal and better. Though our human senses see and taste bread and wine, faith assures that it is the very body and blood of Christ. Cyril has a lovely word for the communioned Christian, *christopheros*, a Christopher, one who bears Christ. Frances Young, the Methodist patristic scholar, has a nice sentence that summarizes Cyril's understanding of what happens in the sacraments, especially in the Eucharist: "The idea of salvation is one of what we might call 'Christification' conveyed in and through the mystery-sacraments."[5] What Cyril is talking about is what Western Christians call "grace," the life of God communicated to us to enfold us in that life. To be divine is to be God, and if God is communicating himself then that communication is divinization. God reaches out from himself to place us within the communion that he himself is. God reaches out to embrace us through the Incarnation and the Eucharist, so that the one reality is dependent upon the other. With this meaning the reception of Holy Communion becomes all important. This is how Cyril describes it: "Approaching, therefore, come not with your wrists extended, or your fingers open; but make your left hand as if a throne for your right, which is on the eve of receiving the King. And having hollowed your palm, received the Body of Christ, saying after it, Amen. Then after you have with care hallowed your eyes by the touch of the Holy Body, partake thereof; taking heed lest you lose any of it; for what you lose is a loss to you as it were from one of your own members . . . Then after having partaken of the Body of Christ, approach also to

---

4. Cyril of Jerusalem, *Mystagogical Catecheses* IV.3.
5. Young, *From Nicaea to Chalcedon*, 131.

the cup of his Blood ... And while the moisture is still upon your lips, touching it with your hands, hallow both your eyes and brow and the other senses."[6] The reality of Christ's eucharistic presence transforms us for and into communion with the God whose being is communion, Father, Son and Holy Spirit.

If Cyril of Jerusalem wrote in Greek for the Christians of the eastern part of the empire, his younger contemporary, St. Augustine of Hippo in North Africa, wrote in Latin, and is the most formative influence on Western Latin theology right down through the Middle Ages. The genius of Augustine's eucharistic theology may be found in a passage from *The Confessions*, a passage that is not immediately eucharistic in meaning, but expresses the nucleus of his understanding. He hears the voice of God-in-Christ saying to him: "I am the food of the fully grown; grow and you will feed on me. And you will not change me into you like the food your flesh eats, but you will be changed into me."[7] This is the same idea as Paul, as Cyril and of countless others before Augustine, ultimately going back to our Blessed Lord himself. But Augustine has the knack of putting it in such a way that it rises up to challenge us. The purpose of the Eucharist for Augustine is to change us into Christ, and as Christ is divine, the purpose of the Eucharist is to make us participate in God.

Augustine's most important reflections on the Eucharist are to be found in his Easter sermons, and so let us proceed to comment on sermons 227, 228, 228B.[8] Sermon 227 is dated to Easter 414–415 AD. The sermon is preached to those who were baptized and received their first Communion the night before. Augustine says to them: "I haven't forgotten my promise. I had promised those of you who have just been baptized a sermon to explain the sacrament of the Lord's table, which you can see right now, and which you shared in last night." The sanctified bread and wine are the body and blood of Christ and, says Augustine, "If you receive them well, you are yourselves what you receive." These neophytes, just received into the church, are provided with the most profound Christian identity. As the eucharistic elements are the very presence of Christ, so are they, if they receive the elements well. Augustine, going on to comment on the order of celebration, comes to the words

---

6. Cyril of Jerusalem, *Mystagogical Catecheses*, V.21–22.

7. St. Augustine, *The Confessions*, 124.

8. Following the order and translation of Hill, *Sermons on the Liturgical Seasons*, 254–72.

"Lift up your hearts . . ." "If you have become members of Christ, where is your head? Members have a head. If the head hadn't gone ahead before, the members would never follow. Where has our head gone? . . . Our head is in heaven . . ." Their union with Jesus Christ, their Head, is absolutely real, and that is the reason why they are invited in the liturgy to lift up their hearts and to reply "We have lifted them up to the Lord." The implications would seem to be that where Christ the Head is they are to follow. Christ's grace is pulling them up, as it were, into the heaven where he dwells with the Father and the Spirit.

In Sermon 228, preached perhaps at Easter 428 AD, Augustine uses the powerful metaphor of birth-rebirth to speak of Baptism and the Eucharist. Addressing the faithful who have been baptized some time, he tells them that their Christian lives should be examples of faith for the newly born in baptism. "What ought to be growing strongly in you has been started afresh in them; and you that are already the faithful must set them good examples which can help them to make progress . . . Being newly born, you see, they look to you to observe how to live, who were born a long time ago." If the faithful are not living as Christ's Body, fed and nourished through the Eucharist, what realistic hope can there be for the infants of the Easter Vigil?

In Sermon 228B Augustine returns to the change effected in believers through eating the Eucharist. "And therefore receive and eat the body of Christ, yes, you that have become members of Christ in the body of Christ; receive and drink the blood of Christ . . . So then having life in him, you will be one flesh with him." Augustine was fascinated by the dual meaning of Paul's "body of Christ" noted above. It referred to the eucharistic gift and to the ecclesial people.

In Sermon 272 he can, therefore, say to the neophytes, "The mystery that you are lies on the table; it is your own mystery that you receive." For Augustine to receive the Body of Christ in the Eucharist is to be received by Christ into his body which is the church. Paul McPartlan, in his excellent book, *Sacrament of Salvation: an Introduction to Eucharistic Ecclesiology*, sums up Augustine's insight in this way: "In other words, the Eucharist makes the Church; we are the real body of Christ, formed into this identity by receiving the Eucharist. The Eucharist is where the church mystically comes into being, hence the Eucharist is the mystical body of Christ. That is a perception which runs through the patristic period, giving the first ten to twelve centuries of Christianity a distinctive stamp.

The church is defined by the sacrament of the Eucharist."[9] McPartlan has surely captured the eucharistic emphasis of this first millennium of Christian faith, but the same emphasis present in different words may be found also in the second millennium. Here we turn for exemplars of this insight to three women, whose mystical writings contain references to the Eucharist that carry on the tradition of the Eucharist making the church.

Hadewijch, Mechthild, Julian

In mediaeval Europe there emerged communities of women known as the Beguines who lived pious and devout lives, sometimes on their own, sometimes in small communities. They were women who wished to live a more evangelical life, but without becoming nuns. Blessed Hadewijch of Antwerp was probably a Beguine, the first great poet in the Flemish language, writing between 1220 and 1240.

She was a well-educated women, versed in the Latin Bible and theology and the liberal arts disciplines of her day. Hadewijch was first and foremost a mystic of Love. God as Love, enabling love in us, brings about our consummation in love. Since the Love that God is became incarnate in Jesus Christ, in his entire Paschal Mystery, loving has what might be called a christic and paschal character, and at the heart of it lies the Eucharist. This is what she has to say about the Eucharist: "And eats his flesh and drinks his blood: the heart of each devours the other's heart, one soul assaults the other and invades it completely, as who is Love itself showed us when he gave us himself to eat, disconcerting all the thoughts of man. By this he made known to us that Love's most intimate union is through eating, tasting, and seeing interiorly. He eats us; we think we eat him, and we do eat him, of this we can be certain. But because he remains so undevoured, and so untouched, and so undesired, each of us remains so uneaten by him and separated so far from each other."[10] This is a truly fascinating passage. "The heart of each devours the other's heart." The soul in love with Christ desires union with him, but that very desire for union is already anticipated by Christ in the institution of the Eucharist. At the foundational moment of the Last Supper, Christ provided the means by which union with him would be achieved. The

---

9. McPartlan, *Sacrament of Salvation*, 36–37.
10. Hadewijch, *The Complete Works*, 110–11.

God who is Love and loves us takes the initiative and is always ahead of us. His desire to be one with humankind is what is enabled and brought about through the Eucharist. Notice how Hadewijch points out the implication of not receiving the eucharistic Christ. When Christ remains "undevoured and undesired," and so we are "uneaten by him," we are separated from the rest of the Body of Christ, the church. Not to participate in the eucharistic Body of Christ makes for separation and division in the ecclesial Body of Christ.

In another passage Hadewijch tells us about receiving Holy Communion one Easter Sunday: "Later, one Easter Sunday, I had gone to God; and he embraced me in my interior senses and took me away in spirit. He brought me before the Countenance of the Holy Spirit, who possesses the Father and the Son in one essence ... A voice issuing from this Countenance resounded so fearfully that it made itself heard above everything. And it said to me: 'With regard to all things, know what I, Love, am in them! And when you fully bring me yourself as pure humanity in myself through all the ways of perfect love, you shall have fruition of me as the Love who I am. Until that day, you shall love what I, Love, am. And then you will be love, as I am Love. And you shall not live less than what I, Love, am, from that day until the death that will make you alive. In my unity, you have received me and I have received you. Go forth, and live what I am; and return bringing me full divinity, and have fruition of me as who I am."[11] One cannot help but notice the eucharistic sequence of the passage. On Easter Sunday, Hadewijch "had gone to God," that is, she received Holy Communion. From that eucharistic union, which, of course, lifts one up into the Trinity—she notes the Father, the Son and the Spirit in the vision—she is sent forth in mission, to act as Love's conduit of love, back to Love as the final term of the mission.

Mechthild of Magdeburg was a younger contemporary of Hadewijch, and probably became a Beguine about 1230 in the city of Magdeburg, Germany. The recipient of many spiritual and mystical experiences, Mechthild was encouraged to put them into writing in her own German language, and her book became known as *The Flowing Light of the Godhead*.[12] Her preferred literary genre is the dialogue or conversation with God. Her theology is experiential rather than speculative, as

---

11. Ibid., 272.
12. *The Flowing Light of the Godhead*.

emerges for example, in these words about the Holy Trinity: "My soul flew to God so swiftly that she literally arose with no effort on her part and snuggled herself into the Holy Trinity, just as a child snuggles into its mother's coat and lays itself right at her breast."[13] It is a lovely image, but its loveliness is rooted in the sheer ordinariness of womanly and maternal experience. The soul wanted the comfort of her maternal God and found it with ease.

Mechthild has a profound sense of her unworthiness to attend Mass and to receive the Eucharist. In a vision she has of the Eucharist unfolding, she sees the church filling with all the ecclesial ranks—saints, apostles, martyrs, angels, blessed souls. Perhaps because of her mediaeval sense of social order allied to her sense of unworthiness to receive the sacrament, she is not quite sure where to position herself. And so she reflects, "Did she stay there in her wretched condition?"[14] This sense of unworthiness, however, does not prevent her going to Holy Communion: "(Jesus Christ) shall I, the least of souls, take in my arms, eat him and drink him, and have my way with him." As the passage continues, she recognizes that not even the angels have this unique eucharistic privilege: "This can never happen to the angels. No matter how high he dwells above me his Godhead shall never be so distant that I cannot constantly entwine my limbs with him, and so I shall never cool off. What then do I care what the angels experience?"[15] In this passage, Mechthild uses the image of marital intimacy to express the union between Christ and the soul in the Eucharist. A God so easily accessible to the soul could not be a distant God.

Julian of Norwich (ca. 1342–after 1413) was an anchoress attached to the church of St Julian in Norwich, in the southeast of England. An anchoress retired from the world to live within the confines of her anchorhold, her church dwelling. Our knowledge of Julian's life is scant. We do not even know her given name, Julian being the name of the church to which she was attached. She tells us that her "Showings" or revelations occurred when she was thirty and a half years old. Her visions were, among other things, of Christ's loving suffering on the cross, and of creation as small as a hazelnut in God's hand, yet utterly loved by God. Her revelations vibrate from beginning to end with the theme,

13. Ibid., 234.
14. Ibid., 74.
15. Ibid., 87.

"Love was his meaning." "And from the time it was revealed, I desired many times to know in what was our Lord's meaning. And fifteen years after and more, I was answered in spiritual understanding, and it was said: What, do you wish to know your Lord's meaning in this thing? Know it well, love was his meaning. Who reveals it to you? Love. What did he reveal to you? Love. Why did he reveal it to you? For love. Remain in this and you will know more of the same. But you will never know different without end."[16]

The Passion of Christ is understood as love, as the supreme manifestation of the love of God. In a sense love for Julian is a way of describing every attribute of God. Love is not something that God does, or expresses alongside other manifestations of his being. All God's actions and all God's being are integrated in love.

Julian writes very little about the Eucharist, but what she has to say is particularly beautiful. To open up her understanding it is necessary to turn first to the entire chapter of the *Showings*. In the chapter she is contemplating the motherhood of God at work. For her there simply is no other relationship that comes closer to expressing God's love for us than motherhood. The image is so organic and all-encompassing for her that she can apply it to Mary, the church, and our natural mothers, as well as to Jesus. The very value of imaging God as Mother for Julian becomes its sheer polyvalence, its ability to encapsulate a range of meanings deeply focused on God's own self. Unlike our earthly mothers who bear us for pain and death, our true Mother Jesus bears us for joy and for endless life.[17] We share that joy and endless life when we are brought to birth by Mother Jesus, and the labor pains of Mother Jesus are the pain and suffering of the cross. From Jesus' writhing in travail upon the Cross the church is born. A child once born needs to be fed and nourished, and Julian tells us that Mother Jesus feeds us with his own self in the Eucharist. The passage is very lovely: "The mother can give her child to suck of her milk, but our precious Mother Jesus can feed us with himself, and does, most courteously and most tenderly with the Blessed Sacrament, which is the precious food of true life; and with all the sweet sacraments he sustains us most mercifully and graciously, and so he meant in these blessed words, where he said: I am He whom Holy Church preaches and teaches to you. That is to say: All the health and

---

16. Colledge and Walsh, *Julian of Norwich, Showings*, 342.
17. Ibid., 298.

life of the sacraments, all power and grace of my word, all the goodness which is ordained in Holy Church for you, I am he."[18] Julian is not the first in the tradition to compare the Eucharist to a mother's milk, but she gives the image her own particular nuance.

Conclusion

Our pilgrimage is over! Two things emerge with utter clarity from our eucharistic witnesses: that Christ is really present in the Eucharistic gifts of his body and blood; and that these gifts are given in order to transform us, through grace into the Giver. The Eucharist as Christ's Body makes the Church Christ's Body. The then Cardinal Joseph Ratzinger, writing in the 1980s, sums up this emphasis that we have found in each of our six representatives: "The church is a celebration of the Eucharist; the Eucharist is the Church; they do not simply stand side by side; they are one and the same."[19] The same point was made by one of Pope Benedict XVI's theological heroes, Henri de Lubac, SJ, writing in 1953: "The church, like the Eucharist, is a mystery of unity—the same mystery, and one with inexhaustible riches. Both are the Body of Christ—the same Body. If we are to be faithful to the teaching of Scripture, as tradition interprets it, and wish not to lose anything of its essential riches, we must be careful not to make the smallest break between the Mystical Body and the Eucharist."[20] Or, in de Lubac's fine phrase, first penned in 1944, "The Eucharist makes the Church."[21]

---

18. Ibid.

19. Ratzinger, *Principles of Catholic Theology*, 53.

20. De Lubac, *The Splendor of the Church*, 156. The book was first published in French in 1953.

21. De Lubac, *Corpus Mysticum*, 88.

CHAPTER NINE

John Donne, Catholicism, and the Eucharist

*Can any of us claim that our motives are unmixed
or even entirely clear to us?*

Rowan A. Greer[1]

A COUPLE OF YEARS ago on the feast of Saints John Fisher and Thomas More a colleague and I fell into conversation focusing on new and fresh approaches to the turbulent history of the sixteenth century Reformation. I remarked that what was going on both in England and in the European continent must not have been entirely clear either to theologians or to ordinary people. My colleague, on the other hand, opined that he thought matters were very clear, that theologians such as Bishop John Fisher and informed laity like Sir Thomas More knew exactly where matters stood, and responded appropriately. I am not seeking refuge in unclarity for its own sake, but I believe that the contexts and circumstances of people are often fragile, that people struggle to do their best with what they've got, and agonize over decisions and positions. I think this was the case, for example, of John Donne, who was born a Roman Catholic but moved over to the Church of England. To say the least, Donne's decision was not impetuous, nor did he entirely leave behind his Catholic perspective.[2]

---

1. Greer, "John Donne, the Sorrowing but Joyful Penitent," 165.
2. Quotations from Donne's sermons are taken from the *Sermons of John Donne*.

John Donne

John Donne (1572–1631) came from a devout recusant family, that is to say, a family that remained Catholic at the time of the English Reformation, and refused to participate in the state-required Sunday services. Two of his uncles, Ellis and Jasper Heywood, became members of the Society of Jesus. Having come to England in 1581 as a missionary, Jasper Heywood was captured and imprisoned in 1583, tried and committed to the Tower of London in 1584. Donne could not have been unaware of this. Given the fact that Donne demonstrates some antagonism towards the Society of Jesus in his "Ignatius His Conclave" of 1611, it is possible that Heywood put some pressure on the young man to join the Society. He studied at Oxford University, and then proceeded to study law at Lincoln's Inn, London from 1592 to 1594. His brother Henry was captured by the authorities in 1593 along with a Catholic priest, William Harrington. Harrington was executed, and Henry Donne died of the plague at London's infamous Newgate prison.

Donne moved from his native Catholicism to the Church of England during his time at Lincoln's Inn. He also moved from the study of law to seeking preferment in service to the court. He had a name as a womanizer and a man about town. After various ventures abroad, 1597 saw him back in London as secretary to Sir Thomas Egerton, Lord Keeper of the Great Seal of England. Through Egerton's household he met Ann More. The two were married in 1601, but since Donne married without the consent of his father-in-law, and further married one who was legally a minor, he was imprisoned for a while, released, but lost his position. From 1602 until ordination in 1615, thirteen long years, the family lived in real poverty. Though Ann More's father had the means he had not the will to help his daughter, her husband and their growing family. During this period, Donne cultivated patrons, gave himself to the study of theology and canon law, and wrote verses.

In 1615 John Donne was ordained priest by the Bishop of London, John King. Preferment at court was still part of his ambition, perhaps part of his proceeding to holy orders, and so he became Chaplain-in-Ordinary to King James I, and he was made Doctor of Divinity of Cambridge University. In 1616 he received the important office of Divinity Reader of Lincoln's Inn. There he made a name for himself as a preacher, and a number of his sermons survive. His wife Ann died in 1617. Anglican historian and theologian, John Booty, writes: "Ann's death provided a significant turning point in John Donne's life. Thereafter he possessed a deepening sense of priestly vocation."[3] About three years before Ann's death, Donne wrote to her brother Sir Robert More, "We had not one another at so cheap a rate as that we should ever be weary of one another."[4] He never married again. Ann's influence on Donne must have been very considerable. This is how it is put by John Moses, a twenty-first-century successor to Donne as Dean of St. Paul's Cathedral in London: "The marriage appears to have been a love match from beginning to end in spite of the years of poverty, separation, disappointment and illness. It is tempting to speculate and to ask if Ann's influence had been a key factor in Donne's greater self-awareness, maturity, even vocation. Certainly there is some consensus among scholars that her death served to deepen Donne's awareness of God, his own sense of the rightness of his vocation, and the intensity of his religious feeling."[5]

The year 1621 saw him appointed Dean of St. Paul's Cathedral. Though now financially secure, probably due to years of scraping by, Donne continued to be anxious about money. His health suffered during this last decade of his life. However, poor health provided some fine writing including "Hymn to God the Father." and "Hymn to God my God, in my sicknesse." During the time of plague in London, he lived with Sir John and Lady Danvers. Lady Danvers was the former Magdalen Herbert, the mother of George Herbert. Two such fine poets and theologians—not to mention Herbert as mystic—must have shared many interesting conversations about God and the things of God.

During the last few years of his life Donne had to contend with illness after illness. He also had to look after his mother, who had remained a Catholic. She lived with him and his household in the deanery of St. Paul's Cathedral. Both died in 1631, his mother in January and he in March. Booty comments: "We do not know how she had adjusted to her son's departure from the faith she held dear, but their life together suggests the possibility of some degree of understanding."[6]

---

3. Booty, *John Donne*, 17. The most accessible collection of Donne's writings is to be found in two excellent anthologies: in the John Booty anthology already noted, and in the more recent anthology, John Moses, *One Equal Light*.

4. Letter: John Donne to Sir Robert More, August 10, 1614, cited in Moses, *One Equal Light*, 12.

5. Ibid.

6. John Booty, *John Donne*, 19.

Between Geneva and Rome

If one takes into account Donne's poetry, his devotional writings and his sermons, it is clear that he viewed the position of the Church of England as a mean between the extremes of Genevan Calvinism and Roman Catholicism. This is how John Moses puts it: "The path between the excesses of Rome and the abstinences of Geneva was one that Donne was well-qualified to pursue. 'We need not climb up seven hills, nor wash ourselves seven times in a lake.'"[7] The seven hills are, of course, Rome and the lake refers to Lake Geneva.

While it is easy to charge him with hypocrisy in abandoning the church of his birth for the Church of England, no one really knows the interiority of another. By making the transition from Rome to Canterbury he would have solved the deep inner problem of divided ecclesial and civic loyalties. There seems to be no *a priori* reason to suspect Donne's motives in this transition, even if in fact it led to greater personal and financial security. Yet, even in his newfound ecclesial allegiance, he probably found himself on particular theological and devotional issues closer to the tradition of Rome than that of Geneva. Thus, John Moses writes: "Nor did he ever distance himself in private devotion or public preaching from the riches of the Catholic tradition of spirituality."[8] In one of his sermons he asks if he is "Papistical", that is attached to Rome, or if he is "Puritan," attached to Geneva. This is his answer: "Men and brethren, I am a Papist, that is, I will fast and pray as much as any Papist, and enable myselfe for the service of my God, as seriously, as sedulously, as laboriously as any Papist . . . Men and brethren, I am a Puritan, that is, I will endeavour to be pure, as my Father in heaven is pure, as far as any Puritan."[9] Through these words and throughout the sermon, arguably, Donne is attempting to reach beyond caricatures of what it means to be a Catholic or a Protestant. Both pledge themselves to God, but differently. While he does not say that the differences are unimportant—and in many other places he establishes what he takes to be the key differences between these Christian traditions—he really does insist that it is the service of God that is *ultimately* important. This God was all important to John Donne. He wrote: "Whom God loves, he loves to the end: and

---

7. John Moses, *One Equal Light*, 29.
8. Ibid., 10.
9. *Sermons* IX.6.395–410.

John Donne, Catholicism, and the Eucharist 93

not only to their own end, to their death, but to his end, and his end is, that he might love them still."[10]

Liturgical Theology

Donne had a very high ecclesiology. The church is the holy body of Christ, animated by the Holy Spirit, ordered by Word and sacraments celebrated by ordained ministers. This is a most important point, as John Booty points out: "While his spiritual journey is profoundly personal, Donne's spirituality is ultimately corporate—the journey takes place in the company of the faithful, the company in which Word and Sacraments are found and the grace to persist on the journey received."[11] The perspective is clearly found in the following passage: "I believe in the Holy Ghost, but doe not find him, if I seek him only in private prayer; But in Ecclesia, when I goe to meet him in the church, when I seeke him where hee hath promised to be found . . . in his Ordinances, and meanes of salvation in his church, instantly the savour of the Myrrhe is exalted and multiplied upon me."[12] There is no disparagement of private prayer in this passage, but it is the liturgical assembly of the Church where the Holy Spirit is best found, animating the Body.

Changing the image of the Church from body to books and libraries, Donne provides a wonderful passage in which he affirms that we are not only bound *to* one another as Church, but bound *into* one another in such a way that the being of one is literally inconceivable without the being of all. In a word, the Church is Catholic:

> The Church is Catholic, universal, so are all her Actions; all that she does, belongs to all. When she baptizes a child, that action concerns me; for that child is thereby connected to that Head which is my Head too, and engrafted into that body, wherefore I am a member. And when she buries a man, that action concerns me: All mankind is of one Author, and is one volume; when one man dies, one chapter is not torn out of the book, but translated into a better language; and every chapter must be so translated; God employs several translators; some pieces are translated by age, some by sickness, some by war, some by justice; but God's hand is in every translation; and his hand shall bind up all our

10. *Sermons* VI. 8. 190–92.
11. John Booty, *John Donne*, 30.
12. Ibid.

scattered leaves again, for that library where every book shall lie open to one another.[13]

This is the beginning of that well-known passage containing the oft-quoted words, "Do not seek to know for whom the bell tolls. It tolls for thee." It is a statement described rightly by John Moses as "incomparable."[14] The entire text is a most lucid and engaging expression of our communion in Christ, and so, therefore, in with and for one another. If we move from the communion that is the Church to the church as a building, we will find no unilateral dismissive position in Donne—"either the people are holy, or the building is holy." Deeply aware of the Catholic sacramental or analogical imagination, *both* are holy: "These walls are holy, because the saints of God meet here within these walls to glorify him. But yet these places are not only consecrated and sanctified by your coming; but to be sanctified also for your coming; that so, as the Congregation sanctifies the place, the place may sanctify the Congregation too. They must accompany one another; holy persons and holy places."[15] Architecture in Catholic liturgical theology, plays neither a sacral nor a merely utilitarian or pragmatic role. It plays a sacramental role, so that the place of worship is best understood as a "sacramental" building. The contemporary Catholic liturgical theologian, M. Francis Mannion, echoes the sentiments of John Donne when he writes:

> Material place symbolically amplifies the liturgical action, and the liturgy, in turn, draws into itself the spatial and material . . . To hold that a church building is simply a functional dwelling is to imply that divine presence is operative no more in a liturgical building than anywhere else . . . Liturgical buildings, on the other hand, should not be conceived of as sacral places, that is, places that limit, contain or bind divine presence and action. God does not dwell exclusively in church buildings . . . I would argue that the more adequate position is that the holiness of the church building and the holiness of the people of God are mutually generative and interactively constitutive.[16]

The assembled church in the church building is made church through Word and Sacrament. The Word is the Holy Scriptures and, most pro-

---

13. "Devotions Upon Emergent Occasions, 1624. Section 7: For whom the bell tolls."
14. John Moses, *One Equal Light*, 53.
15. Sermons IV.15.16–22.
16. Mannion, *Masterworks of God*, 145–47.

foundly, the Holy Scriptures are Christ because Christ is the Word: "Christ spoke Scripture; Christ was Scripture. As we say of great and universal scholars, that they are . . . living, walking, speaking libraries; so Christ was . . . living, speaking Scripture. Our sermons are text and discourse; Christ's sermons were all text: Christ was the *Word*."[17] Thus, Christ the Word speaks the word that he is to and through his body the church. When it comes to the sacraments of the Church, Donne is careful to present a theology of grace mediated by the sacraments but without what he judges to be excessive Roman Catholic sacramental precision:

> The sacraments exhibit and convey grace; and grace is such a light, such a torch, such a beacon, as where it is, it is easily seen. As there is a luster in a precious stone, which no man's eye or finger can limit to a certain place or point in that stone, so though we do not assign in the sacrament, where, that is, in what circumstance or part of that holy action grace is; or when, or how it enters . . . yet whosoever receives this sacrament worthily, sees evidently an entrance, and a growth of grace in himself.[18]

It is not difficult to find Reformation polemics behind this statement on sacramental grace, or how the sacraments cause grace. Donne prefers mystery to explanation. Yet, he has clearly here the Catholic insistence that the sacraments do cause grace, that is to say, effect, sustain and strengthen our communion with God—the one who receives the sacraments "sees evidently an entrance, and a growth of grace in himself." In keeping the liturgy of the Word, especially preaching, in close association with the Eucharist Donne uses the very ordinary analogy of thunder and lightning: "They are a powerful thunder, and lightning, that go together: preaching is the thunder, that clears the air, disperses all clouds of ignorance; and then the sacrament is the lightning, the glorious light, and presence of Christ Jesus himself."[19] Notice that last clause—"presence of Christ Jesus himself." The Eucharist is the very presence of Christ. At a time when theologians in the Church of England and in continental Europe made a battlefield of the Eucharist, it is refreshing to see such a clear statement of eucharistic presence. This clear statement of

---

17. *Sermons* VII. 16.253–57.
18. *Sermons* II. 12.290–301.
19. *Sermons* IV. 3.590–94.

eucharistic presence does not require for Donne an exhaustive and satisfying intellectual analysis, either for himself or for the communicant:

> When you come to this seal of your peace, the Sacrament, pray that God will give you that light, that may direct and establish you, in necessary and fundamental things; that is, the light of faith to see, that the Body and Blood of Christ, is applied to you, in that action; but for the manner, how the Body and Blood of Christ is there, wait for his leisure, if he has not yet manifested that to you: grieve not at that, wonder not at that, press not for that; for he has not manifested that, not the way, not the manner of his presence in the Sacrament, to the Church.[20]

This was the typical position in the Church of England at the time: to affirm the reality of the presence of Christ in the Eucharist, but not to define the mode and the manner of the presence. In some respects this is an unsatisfactory position for a Catholic, given the traditional Catholic emphasis on the "seeking understanding" of the "faith." Yet the fact of that eucharistic presence is clearly believed and expressed and perhaps that is the ultimate value and eucharistic appreciation. This is what Donne is getting at when he says: "The best determination of the real presence is to be sure, that you are really present with him by an ascending faith: make sure your own real presence and doubt not of his . . ."[21] However, in the same sermon from which this quotation is taken he is unnecessarily polemical. "Christ is nearer us, when we behold him with the eyes of faith in heaven, than when we seek him in a piece of bread, or in a sacramental box here." Undoubtedly, Catholics were every bit as polemical in responding to the eucharistic theology of the Reformation traditions, but this kind of negative comment sticks out as quite unnecessary, especially in so fine a writer and firm a believer. Nonetheless, the point needs to be contextualized, something given emphasis by John Moses: "The times in which Donne lived demanded uncompromising statements of conviction. The divide in Western Christendom was too recent, too fundamental, too raw, to encourage the courtesies of a later age."[22] Moses's point is well taken.

From at least the time of the Beguines and early Cistercian women's mystical writing there has been a very close connection between sexual

---

20. *Sermons* VII 11.420–28.
21. *Sermons* VII.4.795–804.
22. John Moses, op. cit., 35.

love and mystical experience.[23] This may also be found in Teresa of Avila and Francis de Sales. John Donne too stands in this tradition. This is the tradition of his "Batter my heart three-person'd God" in which we find these very strong words:

> Take me to you, imprison me, for I
> Except you enthrall me, never shall be free,
> Nor ever chaste, except you ravish me.

He is addressing God in prayer. In that prayer he asks God to ravish him. This strong connection between sexual and erotic language and communion with God is a very Catholic thing. Puritanism may have dimmed it in the popular consciousness, but could never quite eliminate it. It is certainly true that Donne was a very passionate man who composed some very sexually explicit lyrics. But perhaps he has an intuitive appreciation of the Catholic sacramental imagination that enables him to see authentic human sexual love as sacrament of the passionate love of God for us.

One of the most traditional and common gestures in the liturgy of the church as well as in private prayer is the Sign of the Cross. In Donne's time it was often frowned upon by the Puritans, but for him it is a gesture of great power and importance, shown in "The Crosse":

> Since Christ embrac'd the Cross itself, dare I
> His image, th' image of his Cross deny?
> Would I have profit by the sacrifice,
> And dare the chosen Altar to despise?
> It bore all other sins, but is it fit
> That it should bear the sin of scorning it? . . .
> From me, no Pulpit, nor misgrounded law,
> Nor scandal taken, shall this Cross withdraw.[24]

His defense of the sign of the cross—and one could point to numerous other places where he shows an appreciation of traditional Catholic practices—seem to me to point to a Catholicism that remained, even as it was reformed.

---

23. Cummings, *Mystical Women, Mystical Body*.
24. John Booty, *John Donne*, 95.

A Tentative Conclusion

To bring these reflections to a tentative conclusion let us turn to Donne's well-known "A Hymn to God the Father":

> I.
> Wilt thou forgive that sin where I begun,
> Which is my sin, though it were done before?
> Wilt thou forgive those sins through which I run,
> And do run still: though still I do deplore?
> When thou hast done, thou hast not done,
> For, I have more.
>
> II.
> Wilt thou forgive that sin live which I have won
> Others to sin? and, made my sin their door?
> Wilt thou forgive that sin which I did shun
> A year, or two: but wallowed in, a score?
> When thou hast done, thou hast not done,
> For I have more.
>
> III.
> I have a sin of fear, that when I have spun
> My last thread, I shall perish on the shore;
> But swear by thy self, that at my death thy Son
> Shall shine as he shines now, and heretofore;
> And, having done that, Thou hast done,
> I have no more.

In the early 1970s as a young teacher of philosophy, I had a much revered friend and senior colleague, the Irish Jesuit philosopher Joseph O'Mara. Every day of his life Joe O'Mara prayed John Donne's "A Hymn to God the Father." For him it was an act of contrition, as indeed it was for Donne himself. "The spiritual life involved for Donne, in keeping with the times, the cultivation of sincere contrition through self examination in the presence of God and in the context of Scripture and liturgy."[25] This is the very nucleus of life with the God who is Love. We who are so unlovely recognize our unloveliness in God's presence. This is what we witness in "A Hymn to God the Father." The recognition is unavoidable once all pretense has been let go. Donne must have recognized all the particularities of his unloveliness: perhaps his apostasy from Catholicism, the

---

25. Ibid., 25.

pain that he must have caused his devout mother, his lust, and perhaps his pulling his wife Ann into severe poverty with him.

May this act of contrition for Donne have been not only for the quotidian sins in which we all share, but for something more? We know that during the last period of her life Donne's recusant mother lived at St. Paul's Cathedral with her son the Dean. His mother predeceased him by just a couple of months in 1631. What did they talk about during this difficult time? Of course, there is no way to know. It seems to me, however, that matters of faith must have come up between two such devout mother-and-son Christians. Is it possible that behind the sin and the sins of "A Hymn to God the Father" there lies sadness, and perhaps contrition, for the faith-fracture in the Donne family? Perhaps . . .

CHAPTER TEN

P. D. James and Liturgy

God is omnipresent, and life itself is the primal sacrament, namely <u>the</u> visible sign of invisible grace. The structures of our experience are windows into the divine.

John O'Donohue[1]

THIS BOOK BEGAN WITH an attempt to understand prayer as thinking, and then moved on to reflect on various forms of traditional Christian prayer. Newman's life-experience in "Lead, Kindly Light" engaged our attention, before moving on to the arts and to the novelist Graham Greene as resources for theology and spirituality and prayer. Attention then turned to the Eucharist, the very heart of Christian prayer and worship, and to the eucharistic understanding of John Donne, a living synthesis of literature and theology. P. D. James is not a contemporary John Donne, but her fiction has a strong theological and even liturgical ring to it, and she too can be a resource for trying to pray always.

Who Is P. D. James?

Phyllis Dorothy James, now Baroness James of Holland Park, is an English novelist, short story writer, nonfiction writer, essayist and critic. She was born in Oxford, England, in 1920. She attended Cambridge Girls High School but left at the age of sixteen. Her teachers are described

---

1. O'Donohue, *To Bless the Space Between Us*, xvi.

as unabashedly "liberal, Christian, scholarly."[2] In 1941, she married Dr. Connor Bantry White, who was serving during World War II in the Royal Army Medical Corps. He returned from the war suffering from serious mental illness and had to be hospitalized. Ralph Wood writes of this illness in strong terms: "It was as if the outward fear and trembling inherent in the century of mass death had taken inward hold within James's own family." Further, he draws attention to James's description of the very painful marriage between the poet Ted Hughes and his American poet wife Sylvia Plath: "No one who has never had to live with a partner who is mentally ill can possibly understand . . . two people [dwelling] . . . in separate hells, but each intensifies the other.[3]

P. D. James, to support herself and her two daughters, became an administrator for the National Health Service, and after her husband's death in 1964, she moved to the Department of Home Affairs. It was here that she became very knowledgeable about forensic science and police affairs, the backdrop to so many of her novels. In fact, she is best known for her many mystery novels, and especially the central character of Commander Adam Dalgliesh. Among her favorite writers are Jane Austen and Dorothy L. Sayers. Arguably, James has absorbed from the former something of her social and political critique, and from the latter her religious sensibility.

Ralph C. Wood on P. D. James as a Christian Novelist

Few scholars are as well placed as Professor Ralph C. Wood of Baylor University to comment theologically on the work of P. D. James, with feet placed both in the fields of theology and literature. Wood's MA thesis at Texas A&M University-Commerce was entitled "The Scandal of Redemption: Religious Meaning in the Novels of Flannery O'Connor" (1965), and his PhD dissertation at the University of Chicago, directed by the late Nathan A. Scott, Jr. with church historian Martin E. Marty and literary critic Wayne C. Booth as readers, had as its topic "Joyce Cary's Vitalism: A Theological Critique of the First Trilogy" (1975). Wood has published several essays on P. D. James and an interview with her, and he has reviewed a number of her books.

---

2. Cited in Wood, "Deep Mysteries," 960.
3. Ibid., 961.

Wood judges the novels of P. D. James "far more accomplished works of art . . . than the fiction of the much-touted Iris Murdoch."[4] When one takes into account the sheer range of Murdoch's publications both in literature and in philosophy, this is a very high accolade indeed. Although he regards her as a minor figure within the field of contemporary Christian writers, Wood maintains that she is to be found within the grand tradition of Hilaire Belloc, G. K. Chesterton, Ronald Knox, the Oxford Inklings, W. H. Auden, T. S. Eliot, Edwin Muir, Evelyn Waugh, Graham Greene, Georges Bernanos, François Mauriac, Flannery O'Connor, and Walker Percy.

He describes her religious faith as a "spiky kind of Anglo-Catholicism."[5] If "spiky" means something like "sharp," Anglo-Catholicism may be defined as follows: "The name given to the more advanced section of the High Church movement in the Church of England . . . Anglo-Catholics emphasize the dogmatic and sacramental aspects of the Christian creed and life, and the historic continuity of the existing Church of England with that of the Middle Ages . . ."[6] Notice the liturgical note in this description—the sacramental aspects of Christian life. In her book *Death in Holy Orders*, James has a somewhat heated discussion on the nature of theological education and formation for clergy between two of her clerical characters. The Reverend Matthew Crampton, Archdeacon of Reydon, is progressive, while Father Sebastian is more traditional. Archdeacon Crampton: "Unless the church adapts itself to meet the needs of the twenty-first century, it will die. The life your young men live here is ridiculously privileged, totally remote from the lives of the men and women they will be expected to serve. The study of Greek and Hebrew have their place, I'm not denying that, but we need also to look at what the newer disciplines can offer. What training do they receive in sociology, in race relations, in inter-faith cooperation?" Father Sebastian, who presides over a theological college, defends its tradition to the Archdeacon, and then asks him a series of questions: "What is it that you want? A Church without mystery, stripped of that learning, tolerance and dignity that were the virtues of Anglicanism? A Church without humility in the face of the ineffable mystery and love of Almighty God? Services with banal hymns, a debased liturgy and the

4. Wood, "A Case for P. D. James as a Christian Novelist," 583.
5. Ibid., 591. See also Wood, "Deep Mysteries," 961.
6. Cross and Livingstone, *The Oxford Dictionary of the Christian Church*, 58.

Eucharist conducted as if it were a parish bean feast? A Church for Cool Britannia?"[7] It is very tempting indeed to see in these words of one of her characters something of her own thinking about the Church of England and its liturgy.

Ralph Wood writes: "James subscribes to what might be called an incarnational aesthetic: she wants to render the world in all of the fullness and depth, with all of the complexity and horror, that the triune God assumed in becoming flesh within a single human life—not within humanity at large. Just as Jesus was not obviously the incarnate God, so do many of James's Christian concerns remain unstated. They are present more by subtle implication than by overt reference."[8] Her Christian concerns permeate her books and this is particularly true of *The Children of Men*. But it is a subtle and nuanced permeation.

The Children of Men: The Story

The novel to which I wish to address my attention is her 1992 *The Children of Men*. It has been turned into a movie with the same title, but the movie is based very loosely on the book and lacks the detail and sophistication of the novel. James says of this book, not one of her better sellers: "When I began *The Children of Men*, I didn't set out to write a Christian book. I set out to deal with the idea I had. What would happen to society with the end of the human race? At the end of it, I realized I had written a Christian fable."[9] "A Christian fable"—a very accurate description reflected also in the words of Ralph Wood, "a futuristic fantasy, part thriller, part allegory, part cautionary tale."[10] In this book, it is the year 2021 and P. D. James tells the story of the coming extinction of the human race and the baby that just might be its salvation. The baby may be salvific because the entire world has become infertile so that "childlessness becomes a metaphor of godlessness,"[11] The human race is just waiting for the end. "Here indeed is a world in which the conception and birth of a single child could make all the difference."[12]

7. James, *Death in Holy Orders*, 141–42.
8. Wood, "A Case for P. D. James as a Christian Novelist," 586.
9. Wood, "The Mystery of Iniquity," cited from Ralph Wood's website.
10. Wood, "Rapidly Rises the Morning Tide," 279.
11. Wood, "A Case for P. D. James, as a Christian Novelist," 584.
12. Cunningham, *Reading Is Believing*, 70.

One of the central characters is Theodore Faron, a professor of history at Oxford University. He is an intelligent, well-educated but very decided cynic. And with good reason, because humankind is headed for nothingness. His creed can be summed up in his own words: "That once I was not and that now I am. But one day I shall no longer be."[13] It is a very bleak outlook. Not only are there no children, but there is a state sponsored euthanasia program for the elderly who are now unable to make any contribution to this hopeless society. The program is known as *Quietus,* and the people are quiet as, suitably drugged, they are led into boats to the tune of popular songs and the age-old favorite hymn "Abide With Me." The boats are then sunk. Guest-workers are brought into England to do the work that no one else wants to do or can do—they are known as Sojourners—and they are treated in a purely utilitarian and pragmatic fashion. When they are no longer able to do this servile work, they are returned to their countries of origin. Crime is at an all time low because criminals are deported to the Isle of Man in the Irish Sea, which has become for all practical purposes an anarchic penal colony from which there is no return.

A resistance group known as the Five Fishes is attempting to reverse and to subvert these inhumane policies. A member of the group, a woman named Julian, makes contact with Theodore who is related to the Warden of England, his cousin Xan Lyppiatt. The group encourages Theodore to meet with his cousin and to protest these heinous policies, but without success. All that Theodore has managed successfully to achieve is to draw attention to himself from the State Security Police.

Eventually, Theodore joins with reluctance the Five Fishes. In his own way he is in love with Julian who is expecting a baby. A baby! The first baby born in around twenty years could be a wonderful symbol of hope, a new beginning. The first part of the book is called "Omega," the end. The second part is titled "Alpha," the or at least *a* beginning. Theodore is between the old world of Omega and the new world of Alpha, and the bearer of hope is the woman Julian. With her expectant child Julian must be kept out of the hands of the Warden of England so that he may not claim this newborn under the aegis of his tyranny. Without resources, however, this is no mean feat. Theodore pledges to do all he can to enable this birth to happen in real freedom. The other four in the group, apart from Julian, are Rolf (Julian's husband, but not

13. James, *The Children of Men,* 173.

the father of the child), Luke (an Anglican priest, and the father of the child), Gascoigne (a young man of good will but something of a loner), and Miriam (a trained midwife, but who has not delivered a child in two decades). A further description is given by Miriam to Theodore of Luke-the-priest at a later point in the story. Miriam: "You know about Luke. He used to be a priest. I suppose he still is. According to him, once a priest, always a priest. He hasn't got a parish, because there aren't many churches left that want his brand of Christianity." Theodore: "What brand is that?" Miriam: "The sort the church got rid of in the 1990s. The old Bible, the old prayer book. He takes the occasional service if people ask him."[14]

The group drives into rural England, trying to remain inconspicuous, until the baby is born, due at any time. Gascoigne gets caught on some subversive mission. The group is now reduced in number. Rolf abandons the group when he finds out that he is not the child's father, and sets off to warn the Warden of England about the upcoming event in the hope of self aggrandizement. The group is further reduced in number. When they are attacked by an unruly mob of Omegas, young malcontents, the last of the race, born in 1995, who live a life of pillage and killing, Luke allows himself to be caught so as to save the others and especially Julian. He is bludgeoned to death. Only three now remain in the group—Julian, Miriam the midwife, and Theodore.

Theodore finds a place for the birth that seems secure, and Miriam assists Julian in birthing her son. As the novel draws to a close, the Warden of England approaches the place of the birth, intent upon claiming this new birth for his regime, but he meets his death at the hands of his cousin Theodore. Theodore now has the possibility of becoming the political leader. The novel ends with Julian asking Theodore to baptize her son, named after the father and himself, Luke Theodore.

The Children of Men: A Liturgical Reading

Ralph C. Wood writes: "There is no Christianity, James suggests, without strange language and difficult doctrines and unworldly practices Absent such signs of its transcendent uniqueness, Christian faith becomes little more than moral uplift."[15] Central to all this, of course, is the liturgy.

---

14. Ibid., 146.
15. Wood, "A Case for P. D. James as a Christian Novelist," 592.

Speaking of some of her friends, James says that "They love the beauty of the liturgy, though now, alas, it's being increasingly lost, the order and dignity of it."[16]

P. D. James reveals something of her own churchgoing and liturgical practices in the interview with Ralph C. Wood: "The church I often go to, All Saints Margaret Street, is a very fine church in which the Creed and the Gloria are often sung in Latin. They have the Angelus, and they have a professional choir . . . Of course, I think the Eucharist has to be the heart of the action . . . that Holy Communion is the heart of the worship."[17] In her own life she has come out of and she participates in a Christian ecclesial tradition that is centrally shaped and formed by liturgy. In terms of the contemporary situation in England James comments: "People have a belief in God and a great need for God and the need for prayer and the need for God's power, but I don't think they believe the theology of Christianity anymore. I honestly think they don't. They don't really accept the theology of the redemption."[18] My hunch is that James is describing a very real gap between the received tradition of the Church and contemporary human experience. It seems to me possible and eminently desirable to establish a strong positive correlation between the doctrinal tradition of the Church and human experience, but that is not our task here. Our task here is to probe the role and function of the liturgy in this particular novel.

So, what about a liturgical reading of the Christian fable, *The Children of Men*? Whether P. D. James intended her Christian fable to be understood allegorically seems to me to be an open question. However, my liturgical reading of the text will be an allegorical reading in the loose sense of the word. I believe this does justice to the final meaning behind James's Christian fable.

The hero, Theodore Faron, keeps a journal. In this journal he muses about what visitors from other planets might think were they to visit an earth bereft of humankind. As he reflects, his mind turns to St. Peter's Basilica in Rome: "But I like to think of those mythical creatures landing in St. Peter's Square and entering the great basilica, silent and echoing under the centuries of dust. Will they realize that this was once the greatest of man's temples to one of his many gods? Will they be curious about

16. Wood, "The Mystery of Iniquity."
17. Ibid.
18. Ibid.

his nature, this deity who was worshiped with such pomp and splendor, intrigued by the mystery of his symbol, at once so simple, the two crossed sticks, ubiquitous in nature, yet laden with gold, gloriously jeweled and adorned? Or will their values and their thought processes be so alien to ours that nothing at all of wonder will be able to touch them?"[19] Theodore's journal entry expresses an interesting contrast—the splendor of St. Peter's Basilica and the utter simplicity of a cross, the cross of Jesus, albeit he describes crosses that are highly ornamented. Is it possible that, even in a minimal degree, he realizes that the heart of Christianity is the crucified Christ? Of course, he has no overt belief in Christ, nor even in God, but the words of his reflection suggest something. So does his name, Theodore! In Greek it means "gift of God," or it could mean "God gives." Surely a strange name for one who hovers between agnosticism and atheism. That is part of James's methodology; she does not accept that things are black and white, that people are altogether obvious and transparent as good or bad. The human reality is far more complex for James. Later in the novel, Theodore takes a trip across Europe, including a visit to St. Peter's Basilica. He seems drawn to this church, and to the praying that goes on there: "His keenest memory was of Rome, standing before the Michelangelo Pieta in St. Peter's, of the rows of spluttering candles, the kneeling women, rich and poor, young and old, fixing their eyes on the Virgin's face with an intensity of longing almost too painful to witness. He remembered their outstretched arms, their palms pressed against the glass protective shield, the low continual mutter of their prayers as if this ceaseless anguished moan came from a single throat and carried to that unregarding marble the hopeless longing of all the world."[20] It is impossible to believe that a sophisticate like Theodore considered these people as praying to the marble Pieta. No! Behind these words of his describing prayer, there seems to lie some inchoate desire or longing to pray. David Cunningham remarks that "The author develops here the heartbreaking contrast between the present sterile world—in desperate need of a child to save it—and the Virgin Mary, whose child actually does save the world."[21] Theodore experiences something of this heartbreak and that experience arguably is a form of prayer.

19. *Children of Men*, 4.
20. Ibid., 138.
21. Cunningham, *Reading Is Believing*, 74.

This complex Professor Theodore Faron attends Evensong (sung Vespers) on two evenings a week at Magdalene Chapel, Oxford University. It is one of the few chapels still used for worship, and some people have even reverted to using the old Book of Common Prayer. "The choir at Magdalene was among the best regarded and Theo went to listen to the singing, not to take part in an archaic act of worship."[22] This is a curious observation and not at all obvious in its meaning. The text clearly says that Theodore was not worshiping, that he was there to listen to the singing. But surely one might ask, "Why?" What was it about the singing that drew him there week after week? Could it be that the liturgical singing had a transcendent quality about it that raised his mind and heart to something? If that may be judged curious, it is even more curious to know that two of the anthems sung at Vespers were composed by the Catholic and Elizabethan liturgical musician William Byrd, "Teach Me, O Lord" and "Exult Thyself, O God." Not worshiping, Theodore was probably not singing, but these two pieces suggest both a docility to the divine on his part—"Teach Me, O Lord"—and also, somehow, a marvelous awareness of God issuing in praise—"Exult Thyself, O God." An awareness of God is not necessarily conscious. Listening to these doxological words, constantly repeated, *must* do something for the soul. I say "must" because Theodore kept going back. I am asking about the meaning of his going back, and I refuse to accept the premature closure of the issue in the affirmation that he liked it. Liked what? When he meets Julian in the chapel, she knows him because she has come across him in a lecture, but he asks of her: "Julian. That's unusual for a woman. Were you named after Julian of Norwich?"[23] An agnostic/atheist named Theodore who attends the liturgical service of Evensong twice a week, listening to William Byrd, and who knows of Julian of Norwich! Interesting, to say the least.

Theodore's meetings with the Five Fishes normally take place in churches, and the churches all have saints' names. Literary and theological commentator David S. Cunningham makes the obvious connection between the symbolism of the fish, an early Christian symbol for Christ, and the Five Fishes: "The Christian resonances of the name are too loud to escape comment. They try to nourish and feed others; they seek to be

---

22. *Children of Men*, 34.
23. Ibid., 40.

agents of transformation; most of them ultimately die in the process."[24] Why do they meet in churches? Since there are no children, there must have been plenty of abandoned schools and other such buildings in which to meet. So why churches? Perhaps the churches are understood to be holy places where epiphanies of the divine are thought to occur, places where the sacred liturgy is celebrated and God invites humankind to Divine Communion. We are told: "The Church of England, no longer with a common doctrine or a common liturgy, was so fragmented that there was no knowing what some sects might not have come to believe ... The new Archbishop (of Canterbury) ... described herself as a Christian Rationalist ..."[25] The comment reveals a viewpoint that liturgy and doctrine, perhaps even liturgy *from* doctrine, are the bonding agents that make the church. It seems to be implied that these bonding agents, the sacraments and the theology that informs them, continue even when episcopal leadership is not particularly inspiring.

On one occasion, Theodore watches from a distance Luke and Julian at prayer. He soon realizes that Luke has set up a make-shift altar and that he and Julian are celebrating the Eucharist. Theodore remembered some of the liturgical words from church attendance in his childhood.[26] It is an *ad hoc* celebration of the Eucharist, even a primitive celebration, but an entirely reverent and meaningful celebration. Theodore notes the reverence of the celebration—Luke and Julian were "totally absorbed." He notes also some of the ritual moments, for example, the elevation of the eucharistic elements, "the two crumbs," and Julian's preparation to receive the sacrament. He half remembers the eucharistic words from the Book of Common Prayer. Is Theodore growing into the meaning of his name, or perhaps better, is he being led by the gracious mystery of God?

Not long after this celebration, Luke lays down his life to protect the group and especially Julian. Like his Lord Jesus, Luke hands over his life to save others. "Julian said: 'He died to save me. He died to save all of us.'"[27] There is no mistaking the christological shape of these words. When they bury Luke, it has the feel of Jesus' burial. In Luke's case, however, Julian asks Theo to pray the burial service.[28] It is interesting that

---

24. Cunningham, *Reading Is Believing*, 73.
25. *Children of Men*, 68.
26. Ibid., 174–75.
27. Ibid., 186.
28. Ibid., 194.

Theodore was asked to pray the burial service, not Miriam. Perhaps this is James's way of further inducting Theodore into the meaning of his name—"gift of God" or "God gives." The ritual moment for which he is not immediately prepared but is perhaps proximately prepared is truly a moment of grace. Theodore is being changed.

When a suitable place is found for the birth of the baby, it is suggestive of Bethlehem. "Slowly, almost ceremoniously, they entered the shed, heads turning, anxious-eyed, like tenants taking possession of a desired but unknown residence. Miriam said: 'Well, at least it's a shelter and it looks as if there's enough dry wood and kindling here to make a fire.'"[29] Julian's baby is born in a shed, just like another Miriam's baby long ago.

After the tyrannical Warden of England, perhaps suggesting allegorically the wicked King Herod at the birth of Jesus in St. Matthew's Gospel, has been killed by Theodore, a member of his advisory council approaches the newborn baby. His name is Carl and he is dying. This is how the scene plays out: "Carl looked down at the child with his dying eyes and spoke his Nunc Dimittis. 'So it begins again.'"[30] Another Simeon prophesies about another new birth.

The very last paragraph of the novel consists of Julian's request to Theodore to baptize the baby, Luke Theodore:

> "Christen the baby for me. Please do it now, while we're alone. It's what Luke would've wanted. It's what I want." "What do you want him called?" "Call him after his father and after you . . ." There was very little water left in the bottle, but he hardly needed it. His tears were falling now over the child's forehead. From some far childhood memory he recalled the rite. The water had to flow, there were words which had to be said. It was with a thumb wet with his own tears and stained with her blood that he made on the child's forehead the sign of the cross.[31]

Theodore Faron has moved from "interested" listening to Evensong, to observing the Eucharist, to praying the burial rite, to baptizing not just *a* new baby, but *the* new baby, the new Adam, as it were. The story of *The Children of Men* seems to me not only to be a narrative with a strong moral message, not only to be a Christian fable as P. D. James describes it herself, but a Christian narrative that is liturgically shaped. Indeed, the

29. Ibid., 223.
30. Ibid., 240.
31. Ibid., 241.

liturgy in the narrative seems to work *ex opere operato* since Theodore Faron experiences and undergoes what can only be described as conversion, transformation by grace. David Cunningham makes the point that Theo has been brought back by the birth of the baby into the faith of his own childhood.[32] That may be true, but the bringing back, Theo's mystagogical journey, begins at the beginning of the novel. That transforming grace manifested in the new baby has really never been absent.

Conclusion

"Her novels offer a radical alternative to the escapism endemic to most detective fiction, where once the reader has solved the 'mystery' it usually can be forgotten. They confront us, often painfully, with the sinful causes of our crimes. Yet they also hint, ever so joyfully, at their divine remedy. James incarnates these theological insights with such fine artistry that I believe she must be regarded as an important Christian novelist."[33] I hope that Ralph Wood's perspective on Baroness James of Holland Park as a Christian novelist has emerged with some clarity in this chapter. But I hope even more that the centrality of the liturgy in James's outlook has become clearer also, and most especially in *The Children of Men*. And, finally, I hope that P. D. James may encourage us to pray and help us to pray.

---

32. Cunningham, *Reading is Believing*, 77.
33. Wood, "A Case for P. D. James as a Christian Novelist," 595.

CHAPTER ELEVEN

The Eucharist and James P. Mackey

The life-task of the philosopher-theologian consists in a loving reflection on the wisdom carried to him or her in the whole community, in its life and literature, its public liturgy, its developing structures and subsidiary social formations . . .

James P. Mackey[1]

James Patrick Mackey (1934–)

ALTHOUGH HE HAS TAUGHT at the University of San Francisco, it would probably be true to say that the Catholic theologian James Patrick Mackey is not especially well known in the United States. Mackey was born in Ireland in 1934. He attended the national seminary, St. Patrick's College, Maynooth, and went on to receive his Doctorate of Divinity there in 1960, and a second doctorate, in philosophy from Queen's University, Belfast, in 1965. Mackey's teaching career has taken him to Queen's University Belfast, St. John's College Waterford in Ireland, the University of San Francisco, and the University of Edinburgh in Scotland. In Edinburgh he was appointed in 1979 as Thomas Chalmers Professor of Theology in the Faculty of Divinity, an appointment that was controversial in that Mackey was the first Roman Catholic to hold a chair of theology in any Scottish university since the Reformation. After retirement he returned to Ireland, and continues to serve as an honorary

---

1. Mackey, "The Social Role of the Theologian," 42.

professor of theology in the School of Religions and Theology of Trinity College Dublin.

While his theological interests roam over the entire spectrum of systematic and philosophical theology, including Celtic theology, Mackey has never written an entire book on the Eucharist or on worship as such, but throughout his writings there is a strong eucharistic motif, and it bears exploration. This is particularly true of his one-volume systematic theology published as *Christianity and Creation* in 2006. His treatment of the Eucharist in this book but related to his other works will be the focus of this chapter. Mackey's theology is always clear, and yet at the same time, his philosophical acumen and insight often have the mark of poetry. This poetic style invites the reader to a close and personal and enjoyable engagement with his theology. Mackey has some very challenging things to say concerning eucharistic theology and practice. He may even make us feel somewhat uncomfortable. But that is no bad thing because it is too easy to slip into a comfortable complacency about the things of God, and perhaps also into a certain tribalism about the Eucharist. If this consideration of Mackey's Eucharistic theology disturbs our complacency and dislocates our tribalism, then we shall owe him a debt of gratitude.

Spirit and the Eucharist

A key term in Mackey's understanding of God, Christ and the Eucharist is the term "Spirit." This is how he defines it: "(Spirit) connotes a power or force decisive enough to be considered divine, mysteriously beyond all that is constitutive of our empirical world and yet most intimately at work within it."[2] And so the word Spirit, for all practical purposes, comes to stand for the effective but hidden presence of God in creation. Jesus is Spirit-filled—that would be his understanding of the divinity of Christ—and the same Spirit that breathed through the entire Christ event is breathed into us. The Spirit's breathing into us comes centrally through the Eucharist. In and through the Eucharist people encounter the Spirit of Jesus and the Spirit of God, and let it inspire them, that is, literally breathe in and through them. It is, of course the risen Jesus whose Spirit is breathed into us in the Eucharist, and in-breathed by

---

2. Mackey, *Modern Theology*, 80.

this Spirit Christians must breathe the Spirit in turn into the world.³ The liturgy after the liturgy, the mission of the church in the world releases this Spirit-breath of life to invigorate and renew humankind.

Since the Spirit is God, the renewal of humankind that flows from the Eucharist is no merely human effort to ameliorate the human condition. It is the work of grace, to use the traditional code word. It is through the reception of the Eucharist, the in-breathing of the Christ in-breathed, that most especially enables Christians to be grace poured out, broken, and given to all.

Eucharist: Universal Sacrament and Sacrifice

"The eucharistic meal is sacrament and sacrifice to Christian people precisely because it focuses attention on the sacrament and sacrifice of all human meals, and especially on the universal, on-going meal which invites all God's family to the round table of the earth to share in festive mood the abundance of the sustenance for life."⁴ With these words Mackey situates the christological eucharistic sacrament and sacrifice within the horizon of universal sacrament and sacrifice, that is also Spirit-led. All human beings, led by the Spirit, by God present and at work in their lives, find in the very ordinary experience of a meal the effective sign of Spirit at work. Mackey wishes to stress the continuity between creation and what Christians call redemption. He wishes to stress the continuity between the sacramentality of all authentic meal sharing in the sacramentality of the Eucharist. Mackey sees every meal that is thankfully received from God the cosmic Source-Spirit as implicitly Eucharistic.

Mackey has a fine paragraph in which he contrasts the open hand of eucharistic communion with the closed fist of egocentricity.

> Holding the bread in open, chaliced hands, the natural form of the gesture of offering it to others, has the kind of symbolic and effective force that is the very opposite of closing one's hand in on the bread, thus making a fist, and symbolizing and effecting the attempt to secure life and the supports and enhancements of

---

3. Ibid., 83.
4. Mackey, *Jesus the Man and the Myth*, 265.

life by oneself, for oneself, with the constant threat to the lives of others thereby also both symbolized and effective in the fist.[5]

Chaliced hands are open hands, open to receive and to give. Making a fist is closed, defensive and violent. When meals, ordinary human meals are sacramental of Spirit, the hands at those meals are necessarily chaliced hands. Grace is at work, even if it is not named as grace. It is the contrast between receiving eucharistically and grasping egocentrically. This is also the context in which Mackey introduces sacrifice—"the effecting of the sacrifice of each one's life that is necessary for others who live at each other's expense."[6] Sacrifice means a willingness and a commitment to be spent on behalf of others, so that their good becomes primary. Mackey points out, as if it needed to be pointed out, that chaliced hands, not fists, create and overflow with generosity. Chaliced hands make bread multiply for all humankind.

Eucharist: Christological Sacrament and Sacrifice

The description of ordinary human meals as sacramental (that is, Spirit-filled) and sacrificial (that is, costly) leads us to the special meal of the Eucharist. Using the words of Aquinas's hymn, "O Sacrum Convivium" Mackey states that *Christus recolitur,* "Christ is re-called, made present," *mens impletur gratia,* "the participants are filled with the grace of his presence/his spirit," *et futurae gloriae nobis pignus datur,* "they are given a pledge of future glory." The Latin phrases are from Aquinas's hymn. Notice Mackey's comments by way of the progression of thought in this passage. There is the liturgical gathering of people to recall, in the strict scriptural sense of *anamnesis,* the sacrificing and sacrificed Christ. This recalling is around the Eucharistic meal and is, therefore, in the nature of service to others. Grace abounds, that is to say, the Spirit is released from the eucharistic Christ into those who receive him, so that they too become sacrificial in and through this sacrament.

The Eucharist then moves from the level of universal sacramental meal to the level of christological-sacramental-sacrificial meal. The Eucharist takes the universal sacramental meal to more grace filled depth, but a depth that first recognizes the grace of ordinary meals. Just

5. Ibid., 314.
6. Ibid.

as poetry invites us to appreciate the poetic, or shall we say sacral dimension of all speech, so the Eucharist invites us to a depth perception of the sacramentality of meals. Ordinary speech is to poetry as the ordinary meal is to Eucharist. Both are graced but the latter is the mystical depth of the former.

Eucharist before the Eucharist

All Christian traditions that have any appreciation of sacramentality believe the Eucharist to have been instituted by Jesus at the Last Supper. At the same time, it is possible to trace the eucharistic trajectory from the earliest days of Jesus' public mission through to the Last Supper itself. A case in point would be the story of the feeding of the multitude in the Gospels, "in fact and quite unmistakably a story of Eucharist."[7] In St. John's gospel the story opens with those glorious words of Jesus: "I am the living bread which came down from heaven; if anyone eats of this bread he will live forever; and the bread which I shall give for the life of the world is my flesh" (John 6:51). Mackey rightly sees these words as equivalent to the dominical words of institution in the Synoptic Gospels. Close to the beginning of St. Mark's Gospel, after Jesus' baptism by John, Mark describes Jesus sharing a meal with his disciples and with "many tax collectors and sinners" (Mark 2:15–17). Mackey comments that this meal was healing and forgiveness for those who most needed both. The meal was part of the healing. In being invited to the meal the tax collector was invited to discontinue his robbing people, and the prostitute was invited to discontinue damaging herself and others. This is healing.

There is Eucharist before Eucharist, universal Eucharist as it were before christological Eucharist. Meal as sacrament begins biblically in the Garden of Eden where man and woman are invited to eat by God. "The spirit that one breathes in the Eucharistic celebration is the Spirit that came upon creation, according to the first creation myth in the book of Genesis."[8] In Exodus 24:9–11 the covenant, the most fundamental relationship between God and the people of Israel, is sealed with a meal. When the prophets of ancient Israel anticipate "the time when the promises of life will finally be fulfilled," that is the end time, they do so under the symbolism of a meal. Think of Isaiah's feast on the mountain

---

7. Mackey, *Christianity and Creation*, 308.
8. Mackey, *Modern Theology*, 94.

of the Lord when death will be swallowed up (Isaiah 25:6–11). Think of Deutero-Isaiah's feast when people can come and appease their hunger and slake their thirst without money (Isaiah 55:1–5). It is continued in Ben Sira where Wisdom says "Those who eat me hunger for more (all of me), and those who drink me will thirst for more" (Ben Sira 24:21). To partake of Wisdom's Eucharistic Feast is to ingest the Wisdom/Creator Spirit, and so to keep faith with the eternal giver of existence and life. The language is perhaps somewhat unfamiliar to us—"ingesting Wisdom," "ingesting Jesus." The language may be James Mackey's, but the meaning is the tradition of the church going back to Jesus himself at the Last Supper, "Take me, eat and drink me."

Performing the Eucharist

Meal as sacrament and sacrifice and Eucharist as sacrament of sacrifice demands an understanding of the person constantly in service to others. This way of thinking stands in clear contrast to the earliest description offered of the Lord's Supper by St. Paul in 1 Corinthians. Though we find a community fractured and broken in itself at the celebration of the Eucharist, Mackey concludes that St. Paul is "In fact saying that the conspicuous consumerism of some that adds humiliation to the hunger of others, is a sacrament of original sin rather than a sacrament of salvation."[9] Eucharistic appreciation of the other expressed in eucharistic service of the other is the criterion of meal authenticity, of eucharistic authenticity. For him, any meal, wherever it takes place, in symbolizing and effecting the channeling of life to others, is Eucharist. It would be easy to react to such words as reductive of all the traditional Christian understanding of Eucharist. That would miss, I believe, Mackey's real meaning. He is searching for a way of expressing the radical continuity between universal meal and christological Eucharist. It is his way of saying "grace builds on nature." Nature here is the already grace-filled experience of meal; grace here is a fully-filled experience of Eucharist. One may not be hand integrally without the other. This enables Mackey to say: "For in Eucharist the power of gift enables one to die in the most ordinary action of daily life, the meal, in order that that which comes as grace should pass through one's selfless self to others."[10] Mackey is

9. Ibid., 316.
10. *Modern Theology*, 185.

attempting to effect a eucharistic conversion in us the readers. He wishes to avoid at all costs the suggestion that the Eucharist has to do with some "holy huddle," isolated and atomized from the rest of humankind and creation.

This has profound implications. Every dining table and every dining situation takes on a whole new meaning. Every table becomes an altar and chaliced hands that are open to others are both sacrificial and sacramental. There is much food for thought here for sacramental catechesis. Cultivating open, chaliced hands among our children at the table is the experiential foundation for genuine Eucharistic appreciation. Grace building on nature!

Mackey is in this way reaching behind all kinds of controversies about the Eucharist in order to situate the meaning within the contours of ordinary human experience. This is not a denial of what would be called the "supernatural" dimension of the Eucharist. Rather, it is his constant affirmation that grace builds on nature, that there is no nature that is not oriented towards supernature, that those rituals and actions that are most necessarily human are connected intrinsically to those actions through which God is making us divine, providing us with participation in divinity.

Eucharistic Distortions

We have now reached the point in Mackey's understanding of the Eucharist where we may feel somewhat uncomfortable and challenged. Mackey considers that the churches have diverged from the understanding of Eucharist that Jesus had. Divergence occurs when Christian traditions try to possess and to control the eucharistic body of Christ, so that "Only *their* theology of Eucharist, *their* formula, *their* ministry can make Jesus present in the Eucharist."[11] Control such as this prevents the Eucharist as encounter with the risen Lord from becoming life-giving. The most serious of these divergences is to be found, he believes, in the Roman Catholic Church's traditional eucharistic theology. The major divergence has to do in Mackey's judgment with an account of Eucharistic change that is "mystifying" and perhaps "downright magical."[12] In reality Mackey is describing the traditional theology of transubstantiation.

11. Mackey, *Modern Theology*, 85.
12. Mackey, *Christianity and Creation*, 321.

This description of Catholic eucharistic theology is very crude, utterly unsophisticated, and unworthy of Mackey. He is too good a philosophical theologian to fail to recognize the inadequacy of this description to the richness of Catholic eucharistic tradition. This is not to say that there have been no crudities in Catholic expression and understanding. Perhaps such crudities are unavoidable for key Christian doctrines that have come to mean so much to people. Needless to say, Mackey finds the notion of transubstantiation irrelevant and does not hesitate to say so explicitly.[13]

Perhaps he is insufficiently distinguishing the ecclesial doctrine of transubstantiation from scholastic analysis of its meaning. After all, the doctrine of transubstantiation says nothing more than a fair reading of the dominical words at the Last Supper—"This is me." That his real difficulty lies with scholastic theology seems to be clear. He finds such philosophical language abstruse, unrealistic and unpersuasive and, indeed, unintelligible for many "at any level of church membership."[14] Mackey believes that theories like transubstantiation distract from the recognition that what is really present is not the flesh and blood of Jesus' earthly body, but rather the life-giving Spirit that took hold of the historical Jesus and now takes hold of the committed and authentically open Christian community.[15]

However, this seems to me to be very close to what Catholics mean by transubstantiation. Bread and wine are changed into Christ, so that we might be changed into Christ, so that we may be committed and authentically open, so that the world may be christified. Breaking and pouring to each other—Mackey's fine words—is the eucharistic expression of Jesus's axiom about losing life to gain it.

> The clue is contained in the first action of the Eucharistic drama: to take as gift (gratia), to hold in gratitude (gratias agere); for this means, in the words of Gerard Manley Hopkins, to keep grace that keeps all one's goings graces. What is held as gift, be it life itself, is held in permanent openness, to be broken, poured out again in gift.[16]

---

13. Mackey, *Modern Theology*, 74.
14. Mackey, *Christianity and Creation*, 322–23.
15. Ibid., 323.
16. Mackey, *Modern Theology*, 89.

It is a marvelous appreciation of the theology of grace. "Break the bread and give it and pour out the wine. Grace is never so much grace as when it is given again. God the giver of life is never so near, life is never so much as gift, as when one ceases to hold on, to grasp and pull at it, and lets go, for greater love than this no one has."[17]

Mackey turns to another divergence or distortion of Jesus' original Eucharist. It is the idea that participants should be "in the state of grace" before receiving the Eucharist. In disallowing communion to those who are judged not to be in the state of grace, the Catholic Church distorts the healing dimension of the Eucharist as Jesus understood it. The Eucharist is intended to heal sinners. This runs counter to widespread perceptions, and yet the healing dimension of Jesus' meals, and most especially at the Eucharist, is a plain fact. Pastors know this all too well, but there is sometimes a reluctance and resistance to its public acknowledgment.

In a similar way, Mackey places the issue of eucharistic sharing with members of other Christian traditions. When the refusal to share the Eucharist with such others "on a variety of grounds but all of which involve accusations of failures or betrayals in Christian belief or practice, then one is seeing the further damaging, rather than the salving of whole churches."[18] When Christians refuse to share the body of the Lord at the table of the Lord, "it is clear that the spirit of reconciliation is being smothered alive, and that no Eucharistic theology or theory of Eucharistic presidency can compensate for the deadly damage that thereby continues to be done to the crippled body of Christ."[19] Because Christians do not share the Eucharist the body of Christ is crippled. Difficult and very challenging language. I suppose ultimately that Mackey's position poses the question to each of us, "How strong is my passion for the unity of Christ's holy Body, the Church?"

If ecclesial distortion of Jesus' Eucharist is so massive and so widespread, what are ordinary Christians to do? They might go back to earliest Christian practice and celebrate their own Eucharist in their homes, presided over by the mother or father of the family. Again, they might participate but with their own understanding in their local, duly authorized celebration. Or again, they might celebrate the Eucharist in churches of different Christian denominations. Some people do this.

17. Mackey, *Jesus the Man and the Myth*, 161.
18. Mackey, *Christianity and Creation*, 325.
19. Mackey, *Modern Theology*, 91.

Or, should Christians judge the eucharistic distortion to be so complete and beyond reform, they should "just take their food and drink together in the true spirit of gratitude that greets any gift, and break and pour out to each other, and sometimes at least open their table to the poor, and sometimes even to the rich who have done them wrong, and thereby experience in all of this the presence of the living Spirit flowing through them."[20]

Conclusion

Having come to the end of this exposition of James Mackey's eucharistic theology, what does it have to offer us? First, he shows us the importance of rooting the particularity of Christian sacrament in universal human experience. This is very important because there can be too much of a disconnect between ritual and actual human living. Second, he underscores what the Eucharist must mean for us in breathing the Spirit of Jesus, the Spirit of God, into the world through our moral performance. Third, he challenges us to take with the greatest seriousness our ecumenical divisions. One commentator whose words are to be found on the back cover of *Christianity and Creation* has this to say: "Many churches and particularly the Roman part of the Catholic Church, will hate and fear this book. But its scholarship and insights will water the souls and minds of many people. It will also guide a healthy and life-giving religious debate." Hate and fear, no! Watering souls and minds and giving rise to healthy debate, yes!

---

20. Mackey, *Christianity and Creation*, 325–26.

CHAPTER TWELVE

Eucharistic Absence

Introduction

IN A RECENT COLLECTION of his poetry the Irish poet and Nobel laureate Seamus Heaney included a piece about the Eucharist entitled "*Like everybody else . . .*"[1] The poem narrates a familiar experience for Catholics, at least for many Catholics. "Like everybody else," Heaney describes Catholic eucharistic piety—bowing the head during the consecration, raising the eyes at the elevation of the eucharistic gifts, receiving Holy Communion, making it a personal prayerful thanksgiving with eyes closed. He demonstrates an awareness of what is going on during the celebration—"a change occurred"—and he acknowledges mystery. We can all easily identify with this poetic description. In the second part of the poem Heaney appears to be describing what we have come to call "a loss of faith." How he puts it is most interesting. There was no debate within himself nor, indeed, with someone else. Rather, "The loss occurred off stage." The loss of his eucharistic faith did not occupy a central place on the "stage" of his life journey. No, "The loss occurred off stage." That is to say, the loss, at least initially, seemed to go unnoticed. And yet finally Heaney affirms that the traditional eucharistic words and terms—"thanksgiving," "host," "communion bread"—retain a strong and perduring appeal for him. These words "have an undying tremor." There is behind them the deep *mysterium tremendum et fascinans*.

---

1. Heaney, *District and Circle*, 45.

"We Cannot Live without the Lord's Supper"

In his apostolic exhortation, "The Sacrament of Charity," Pope Benedict XVI draws our attention to the martyrs of Abitinae in North Africa: "At the beginning of the fourth century, Christian worship was still forbidden by the imperial authorities. Some Christians in North Africa, who felt bound to celebrate the Lord's Day, defied the prohibition. They were martyred after declaring that it was not possible for them to live without the Eucharist, the food of the Lord."[2] It is a beautiful expression of the centrality of the Eucharist to Christian life—"We cannot live without the Eucharist."

However, an increasing number of Christians today seem to be able to do just that, to live without the Eucharist. Yes, it is possible to live one's life, to get on with one's life without regular participation in the Eucharist. But I want to argue in this chapter that one's life is poorer from deliberate and chosen eucharistic absence. Indeed, if this were not argued, the entire reality of Christianity would vanish. The Eucharist is necessary to living, but in what sense? One way of putting it is to recall the words of the second century bishop, Irenaeus of Lyons: "*Gloria Dei, vivens homo,*" "The glory of God is the human person fully alive." The operative word here is not "alive" on its own, but rather "*fully* alive." There are degrees of being alive, different intensities of vitality. Or, to put it in Irenaeus's terms, we will recognize degrees of vitality centered on the Eucharist.

Why the necessity of the Eucharist? Because the Eucharist goes back to Jesus himself. This is God's chosen way to divinize us, to provide a share in God's own life. We could not be more fully alive than then when we are living with the Jesus life, the eucharistic life in us. That is what our faith tells us. Inquiring Christians, however, look also for reasons. Is there a reason for the centrality and necessity of the Eucharist? Yes, because the Eucharist goes straight to the heart of what it means to be human. The Eucharist, if you will, rehearses in its very ritual what it means to be human, or what it means to be fully alive. The fundamental constitutive elements of what it means to be human, or fully alive, are ritually laid out for us in the Eucharist, and thus, participation in the ritual also enables a deeper perception of our humanity and of vitality.

---

2. Pope Benedict XVI, *The Sacrament of Charity*, par. 95.

The fundamental constituent elements of what it means to be human are: assembly, listening and speaking, eating and drinking, dismissal. "Assembly" affirms that we are essentially social or relational beings. Very obviously, our life in this world comes to be through others, literally through their assembly. In fact, everything that is significant about us as human beings is dependent on our inter-relating with others, or, in my terms on "assembly." One theologian, George Pattison, puts the point very finely: "We are, it may be said, loved into selfhood. We are not only not islands, we never were... 'I' is itself a learned word."[3] Acknowledging our radical relationality demands the consequent acknowledgment that everything is gift. Gift is the principle on which God has based human existence. Everything comes to us as gift—life itself, our nurture, our education as others share human wisdom with us. We in turn then make our own gift-like contribution to the lives of others. Thus, assembly and gift go together.

Listening and speaking come next in this description of what it means to be human. Much of our life is about listening. There is a marvelous passage from the philosopher and literary critic Kenneth Burke that captures the listening dimension of our lives:

> Imagine that you enter a parlor. You come late. When you arrive, others have long preceded you, and they are engaged in a heated discussion, a discussion too heated for them to pause and tell you exactly what it is about. In fact, the discussion had already begun long before any of them got here, so that no one present is qualified to retrace for you all the steps that had gone before. You listen for a while, until you decide that you have caught the tenor of the argument; then you put in your oar. Someone answers; you answer him; another comes to your defense; another aligns himself against you, to either the embarrassment or gratification of your opponent, depending upon the quality of your ally's assistance. However, the discussion is interminable. The hour grows late, you must depart. And you do depart, with the discussion vigorously in progress.[4]

In this passage Burke draws attention also to speaking, but notice the primacy given to listening. There cannot be, quite literally cannot be any speaking without listening. Everyone learns to speak first by listening.

---

3. Pattison, *The End of Theology*, 44–45.
4. Burke, *The Philosophy of Literary Form*, 110–11.

Eating and drinking are obviously basic to human life and require no real comment. Without eating and drinking we cannot live. And yet here too the fundamental dimension of relationality comes into play. Our food is produced together and eaten together. Togetherness is essential. One may take this insight further: "With food we tell one another that we love one another, that we are dependent upon one another, that we desire the other to live and be well."[5]

Finally, there is dismissal. Once one stage of life is complete, life dismisses us, sends us forth and on to the next stage. The womb dismisses us at the time of birth; we are dismissed from the family, in a sense, when we move on to the stage of schooling. We speak of "graduation" from schooling, that is to say, about taking the next *gradus* or "step." We are dismissed from employment when we move on to retirement, and then finally our life in this world comes to an end. There are many endings before *the* end, in each of which we have an experience of being sent out, of being dis-missed.

So, if one would grasp what it means to be human, one needs to take hold of these fundamental constitutive elements. Being human has to do with assembly, listening and speaking, eating and drinking, and dismissal. Those fundamental constituent elements of what is to be human are precisely the choreography of the celebration of the Eucharist. There is no private Eucharist just as there is no private person. Relationality is intrinsic to Eucharist. There is no Eucharist without assembly, not just the empirical assembly of those visibly present, but including the heavenly assembly of the angels and the saints. Once the assembly is assembled, we listen and speak. We listen to the great narratives of the liturgy of the Word, a listening like all authentic listening that is not passive but intensely active. This listening leads us to discovery of God, and in a sense to self discovery as we hear about the vast and variegated human congerie that make up the biblical story. We speak in response in words of prayer and psalmody, in hymns. We move on to eat and drink. Fed through active listening at the Table of the Word, we move on to eat and drink at the Table of the Eucharist, "the twinned tables in the refectory of the Incarnate Logos, one for his word, the other for his flesh."[6] Finally, after eating and drinking, we are dismissed. "The mass is ended. Go in peace." We are sent forth, dismissed to be in the world what we have

---

5. Driscoll, *What Happens at Mass*, 64.
6. Nichols, *The Service of Glory*, 57.

further expressed and become in the assembly, the Body of Christ. We are dis-missed to be that Body in our circumstances, in our place. Thus we recognize the correlation between the description of what it means to be human and the ritual choreography of the Eucharist.

"The Loss Occurred Off Stage"

What about those who can seem to live without the Eucharist? How can we help them to understand that they lose something important and significant through their absence? How can we help them grasp something of Irenaeus of Lyons's *vivens homo*, "the human person fully alive." Seamus Heaney's poem has the title "Like everybody else . . ." The assumption is that his eucharistic experience was much the same as everyone else's. Perhaps we might add that it is a common assumption that eucharistic doctrine, piety and practice have been solidly uniform throughout the entirety of the Christian tradition until our own troubled days. Without in any sense detracting from the pastoral challenges of today, it is important to recognize that there have often been challenges to regular and popular participation in the Eucharist. The challenges did not begin in our time. Recall some words spoken in 1962:

> In the daily exercise of our pastoral office we sometimes have to listen, much to our regret, to voices of persons who, though burning with zeal, are not endowed with too much sense of discretion or measure. In these modern times they can see nothing but prevarication and ruin. They say that our era, in comparison with past eras, is getting worse and they behave as though they had learned nothing from history, which is, nonetheless, the teacher of life.

These words come from Pope John XXIII at the opening of the first session of Vatican II.[7] They are as relevant now as they were then. Or recall some words uttered in the nineteenth century:

> This is a world of conflict, and of vicissitude amid the conflict. The church is ever militant; sometimes she gains, sometimes she loses; and more often she is at once gaining and losing in parts of her territory. What is ecclesiastical history but a record of the ever-doubtful fortune of the battle, though its issue is not doubtful? Scarcely are we singing Te Deum, when we have to turn to

---

7. Cited from Trevor, *Pope John*, 80.

our Misereres: scarcely are we in peace, when we are in persecution; scarcely have we gained a triumph, when we are visited by a scandal. Nay, we make progress by means of reverses; our griefs are our consolations; we lose Stephen, to gain Paul, and Matthias replaces the traitor Judas. It is so in every age; it is so in the nineteenth century; it was so in the fourth.[8]

These words come from John Henry Cardinal Newman, introducing his sketches of church history. Pastoral challenges are with us always.

One thinks of the schismatic situation of the early Corinthian community described by St. Paul in his First Letter to the Corinthians, noted in chapter eight. This earliest Christian description of the Eucharist, some twenty years or so after the Resurrection of the Lord, shows a community singularly challenged about "discernment of the body," discernment most especially about the ecclesial body of Christ.

If we move to Sunday in St. Augustine's Hippo in the early fifth century, then here too we will find significant eucharistic challenge. Recall the marvelous passage about the Sunday Eucharist in Frederik Van Der Meer's *Augustine the Bishop*:

> It is a cool Sunday morning; a continuous muffled noise echoes through the white capital city, except for the ascetics and for those who are both free and well-to-do, there is little in the nature of Sunday rest from servile tasks. Slaves trot through the back streets, the shops are open and the market gardeners and muleteers watch the faithful go up to the great church ... Bishop Aurelius Augustinus, with his flaming dark eyes and shaven head, is at this moment sitting in the *secretarium* surrounded by his clergy, and is just concluding his short morning audience, which he is in the habit of giving before Mass ... Then Augustine follows a long row of assistants, passes under the updrawn curtain between two pillars and ascends the apse ... The doors still stand open and still the people stream in, but now there is a sudden silence, and from the steps of the apse Augustine greets his people. "The Lord be with you." "And also with you."[9]

This word picture of Augustine's church on a Sunday morning is so well drawn one can almost see it! But notice also what Van der Meer is saying—not everyone is going to Mass. Sunday morning is much like

---

8. Newman, *Historical Sketches*, vol 2, p. 1.

9. Van der Meer, *Augustine the Bishop*, 388–89, cited in Cummings, *Eucharistic Doctors*, 74.

any other work day morning for many people. It would seem that not the entire community is present, nor indeed could it be present. This is how a recent biographer of St. Augustine, James J. O'Donnell, describes the situation: "Augustine's own largest church in Hippo at its greatest extent was about 120 feet by 60 feet inside. Even if we make allowances for standing-room only crowds, it could scarcely have held more than a tiny fraction of the population of the city. Who attended? The argument that presents itself most obviously is that the congregation was made up of the upper classes of landowners, merchants, and officers, and that the bulk of the Christian population made do without the weekly inoculation of ritual."[10]

Yale historian of the Roman Empire, Ramsay MacMullen, confirms this perspective. Having examined the great preachers of the latter half of the fourth century, and paying particular attention to the details of their homilies as well as to such data as are available about church buildings, he reaches the following conclusion: "In no city was the church (or world of churches, plural) able physically to accommodate at one time any large majority of the total resident population, even after several generations of post-Constantinian growth of congregation and ecclesiastical building. It was a selection that came to worship, just as it had always been a selection (quite tiny) that attended Roman popular assemblies."[11]

Let us move on some 800 years or so to Humbert de Romans, a Dominican who died in 1277 after a very busy pastoral career.[12] Through his sermons we are presented with a picture of the very ordinary people of his day. Humbert rails against their obsession with money and sex. He comments on their ignorance of the faith. He speaks of those who are obdurate and who "turn away their ears" when Christ is mentioned. He tells us that there are people who "rarely pray during the day," seldom or never attend church, and, if they do, it is once a year for the Eucharist. And even among those who do come for the Eucharist, there are some who do not stand for the proclamation of the gospel or do not sign themselves with the cross. These are some of the eucharistic challenges in this century that

10. O'Donnell, *Augustine*, 31–32. See MacMullen, "The Preacher's Audience," 503–11.

11. MacMullen, "The Preacher's Audience," 510.

12. The following examples are taken from Alexander Murray, "Religion Among the Poor in Thirteenth Century France," 285–324.

produced the outstanding eucharistic theology of St. Thomas Aquinas. The point of these examples, and examples could be culled from the entire history of the Christian tradition, is not to induce or to confirm a sense of pastoral complacency about eucharistic attendance and participation. The point is to recognize that there is no golden age in the observance of the Lord's Day and in the celebration of the Eucharist.

Eucharistic Absence

Having acknowledged something of an historical perspective, it remains for us now briefly to engage the phenomenon of absence from the Eucharist. This is a complex and multifaceted challenge and at most, I can offer here but a few personal thoughts that only begin to address the issue. Immediately, I want to see the absence of Christians from the Eucharist as a challenge for us who cannot live without the Eucharist. I wish to dissociate myself from the perspective of those who are dismissive of the eucharistic absentees who nonetheless remain our sisters and brothers. This is the dismissive attitude of those who maintain, and sincerely maintain that the church "needs to be trimmer and purer." My alignment is with those who think that "the church is a family, and a family keeps embracing even when members don't come home a lot."[13]

Having worked in a quasi-chaplain mode for decades with young people in university, the Irish Jesuit theologian, Michael Paul Gallagher, SJ writes: "The problem is that many people have encountered the Christian vision only in tired language and in frozen forms. The hope here is to awaken the sleeping beauty of our wonder so that we can be more ready for the greater wonder that is Jesus Christ."[14] The majority of people around who are absent from regular contact with the church and the Eucharist seem not to do so because of some intellectual argument against their Christian faith. Rather, they seem to have drifted away because their imagination, and perhaps also their loves and hopes have been untouched by the community of the church and the experience of the Eucharist. It is not so much a matter of blame. Society produces for us opportunity, virtually endless amusement, and what might be called "thick" distraction.[15] There is no obvious and immediate panacea for

---

13. The words come from Rohlheiser, "Knock It Off," 15.
14. Gallagher, *Dive Deeper*, 4.
15. Adapting some thoughts from Rohlheiser, "Knock It Off," 15.

eucharistic absence. Perhaps people have to experience great vulnerability before thinking seriously about God, church, Eucharist. Perhaps also we might respond on two levels.

On one level, we might seek to explore the pre-theological or the pre-religious reflective experiences of such persons. It needs to be recalled that God is ahead of us in this, that God is never absent and that people are incessantly being lured by this passionate loving God even when they do not recognize him nor name him. Michael Gallagher puts it like this:

> We have an inner core of Spirit-guided desire before we arrive at explicitly Christian interpretations of our experience. Our hearts are being drawn towards love prior to finding the face of Love in Christ. There is a risk of rushing into the world of explicit religion without pausing on what is more fundamental in each of us—the experience of searching, of struggling to live genuinely, of being slowly transformed by the adventure of life. Here in silence and even in secret we are being shaped as lovers.[16]

If we as church, as those who cannot live without the Eucharist, were seriously to engage our sisters and brothers who are not with us, were seriously to *listen* to them—in their searching, in their struggle to live genuinely, in the slow process of transformation, *without any manipulation*—and if we lived out our understanding of the Eucharist more fully at both the theological and divine level as well as at the anthropological level, who knows what might happen? Perhaps we need to develop our capacity to be surprised by grace as much as we need to produce better programs to induce Christians to return to the eucharistic community. If active listening is constitutive of what it means to be human, then *a fortiori* there is a need to listen to those whose lives are not explicitly eucharistic. The satirist and author Tony Hendra makes this comment: "The only way to know God, the only way to know the other, is to listen. Listening is reaching out into that unknown other self, surmounting your walls and errors; listening is the beginning of understanding, the first exercise of love." He learned the importance of the virtue of listening from the English Benedictine, Dom Joseph Warrilow, his spiritual mentor. Dom Joseph said to Hendra: "None of us listen enough, do we dear?

---

16. Gallagher, *Dive Deeper*, 120.

We only listen to a fraction of what people say. It's a wonderfully useful thing to do. You almost always hear something you didn't expect.[17]

Circles of Engagement

On a second level, we might recognize that any living eucharistic community is made up of concentric circles of commitment and encounter. One author refers to "circles of engagement": "People engage with church at different levels and the intensity or otherwise of this engagement is dependent on many factors . . . In exploring this it may be appropriate to look at engagement in terms of circles rather than levels, 'circles of engagement.'"[18] The pastoral response is to meet these people within their own circle of engagement with a welcome and an openness. We might speak of four circles of engagement. First, is the inner circle, the circle of the true believers whose participation in the church is central to their self understanding. "This is the heart of the church, the community that holds the center. The church has no choice but to devote its primary energy to the life and sustenance of this particular circle of belonging because this is the center and it must hold. The furthest reaches of the periphery need the center because without the center there is no periphery." In our terms these are the people who cannot live without the Eucharist. Second is the circle of human and spiritual connection. This is a large group of people, who regard themselves as spiritual, and yet do not feel the need, for whatever reason, to participate fully in church or the Eucharist. They often describe themselves as spiritual but not religious. What if pastoral encounter with such people took the shape of a receptive seeking to understand without any immediate expectations? Third is the circle of consolation. "People are fragile and they need a place beyond home, hospital and clinic where they can take their brokenness, their loneliness or their grief to have it soothed among hymns and candles and psalms and scent. They may simply need to sit in silence or be in the warmth of a crowd . . . They simply want a space, a space populated or unpopulated where they can find gracious consolation. The church can offer such space in a way that most other agencies, bodies and organizations cannot." This is a pressing need for most people, the circle of consolation, and those who cannot live without the

---

17. Hendra, *Father Joe*, 181.
18. O'Brien, "The Church: Circles of Grace," 141–43.

Eucharist, bodied and blooded with Christ in Cyril of Jerusalem's terms, are well-placed to be the place of consolation. Fourth, the circle of ritual. "People need ritual to mark the significant times like birth, marriage, illness, partings and death and this is an area in which the church has real wisdom, experience and expertise. It has enormous richness and beauty and its rituals of passage. It marks and honors the significant milestones of life with grace, depth and elegance in ways that opened people to a deeper sense of what it means to be a human being." There is a school of thought that believes access to the church's rituals should really be for the fully participant members of the church, for circle one. This seems very shortsighted and exclusive.

Graciousness on the church's part and the use of imagination when it comes to providing ritual for non-practicing members of the broader community is one of the greatest services the church can offer to that community. This gracious sharing of the church's expertise and experience in honoring the significant moments of life could paradoxically be a space of real witness and evangelization.[19]

The then Cardinal Joseph Ratzinger, in an extended interview with the journalist Peter Seewald made the following comment: "I have nothing against it if people who all year long never visit a church go there at least on Christmas Night or New Year's Eve or on special occasions, because this is another way of belonging to the blessing of the sacred, to the light. There have to be various forms of participation and association; the Church has to be inwardly open."[20] This is "circles of engagement" thinking about the church. Liturgical-sacramental-ecclesial growth can no more be demanded than psycho-social growth. A welcoming ecclesial attitude optimizes in every way possible the movement and development from mere physical location in and around the church's rituals—if there is such a thing as mere physical location!—towards conscious choice for ecclesial and sacramental participation.

Conclusion

The concluding sentence in Seamus Heaney's poem is: "They have an undying tremor and draw, like well water far down." The "they" refers to eucharistic words—"thanksgiving," "host," "communion bread." Could

19. Ibid., 143.
20. Ratzinger, *God and the World*, 442.

these same words not apply also to the eucharistic assembly? Could the eucharistic assembly not also be described appropriately as "eucharistic thanksgiving," "eucharistic host," "eucharistic bread"? It is the challenge of the eucharistic assembly so to live these words that the tremor and the attraction/drawing will continue to be experienced among the people from whom Christ is never absent, even if they are absent from the assembly. The water may be far down the well, but we cannot live without it.

Bibliography

Ashton, John, "Abba," in David N. Freedman, ed., *The Anchor Bible Dictionary*, vol. 1 (New York: Doubleday, 1992), 7–8.
Augustine, St., *The Confessions*, tr. Henry Chadwick (Harmondsworth: Penguin Books, 1991).
———. *Sermons on the Liturgical Seasons*, tr. Edmund Hill (New York: New City Press, 1993).
Baldovin, John F., *Bread of Life, Cup of Salvation* (Lanham, MD: Rowman and Littlefield, 2003).
Barron, Robert, *The Strangest Way* (Maryknoll, NY: Orbis Books, 2002).
Begbie, Jeremy, "The Gospel, the Arts and Our Culture," in Hugh Montefiore, ed., *The Gospel and Contemporary Culture* (London: Mowbray, 1992), 60–74.
Benedict XVI, Pope, *The Sacrament of Charity* (Washington, DC: USCCB, 2007).
Bierman, Lisa C., "Scobie Reconsidered: A Casualty of Catholicism or Conscience?" *Renascence* 55 (2002), 65–77.
Blehl, Vincent, *Pilgrim Journey, John Henry Newman 1801–1845* (New York-Mahwah, NJ: Paulist Press, 2001).
Bondi, Roberta, *A Place to Pray* (Nashville: Abingdon Press, 1998).
Booty, John, ed., *John Donne, Selections from Divine Poems, Sermons, Devotion and Prayers* (New York-Mahwah, NJ: Paulist Press, 1990).
Bouyer, Louis, *Newman, His Life and Spirituality* (New York: P. J. Kenedy & Sons, 1958).
Brown, Raymond E., *The Gospel According to John 1–12* (Garden City, NY: Doubleday, 1966).
Brueggemann, Walter, *The Message of the Psalms* (Minneapolis: Augsburg, 1984).
Burke, Kenneth, *The Philosophy of Literary Form*, 3rd ed. (Berkeley: University of California Press, 1973).
Casarella, Peter, "Contemplating Christ Through the Eyes of Mary," *Pro Ecclesia* 14 (2005), 161–73.
Countryman, L. William, *Forgiven and Forgiving* (Harrisburg, PA: Morehouse Publishing, 1998).
Cross, F. L. and Livingstone, E. A., ed., *The Oxford Dictionary of the Christian Church*, 2nd ed. (New York and London: Oxford University Press, 1974).
Cummings, Owen F., *Eucharistic Doctors* (New York-Mahwah, NJ: Paulist Press, 2005).
———. *Mystical Women, Mystical Body* (Portland: The Pastoral Press, 2000).
Cunningham, David S., *Reading Is Believing: The Christian Faith Through Literature and Film* (Grand Rapids: Brazos Press, 2002).
Dahood, Mitchell J., *Psalms 1–50* (Garden City, NY: Doubleday, 1965).

Daley, Brian E., "How Should We Pray? Five Guiding Principles," *Crisis* 12 (1994), 28–32.
Davie, Donald, ed., *The New Oxford Book of Christian Verse* (New York and Oxford: Oxford University Press, 1988).
Dicharry, Warren, *Praying the Rosary* (Collegeville: The Liturgical Press, 1998).
Driscoll, Jeremy, *What Happens at Mass* (Chicago: Liturgy Training Publications, 2005).
Duffy, Eamon, *Faith of Our Fathers* (New York and London: Continuum, 2004).
Finn, Thomas M., *From Death to Rebirth: Ritual and Conversion in Antiquity* (New York-Mahwah, NJ: Paulist Press, 1997).
Gallagher, Michael P., *Dive Deeper: The Human Poetry of Faith* (London: Darton, Longman and Todd, 2001).
Gorringe, Timothy, *Discerning Spirit* (London: SCM Press, 1990).
Graef, Hilda, *Modern Gloom and Christian Hope* (Chicago: Henry Regnery Co., 1959).
Gray, John, "A Touch of Evil: Graham Greene," *New Statesman*, November 27 (1996), 37.
Greeley, Andrew M., *The Catholic Imagination* (Berkeley: University of California Press, 2000).
Greene, Graham, *The Heart of the Matter* (Harmondsworth: Penguin Books, 1999).
Greer, Rowan, *Christian Hope and Christian Life* (New York: Crossroad, 2001).
Hadewijch, The Complete Works (New York-Ramsey-Toronto: Paulist Press, 1980).
Heaney, Seamus, *District and Circle* (New York: Farrar, Strauss and Giroux, 2006).
Hendra, Tony, *Father Joe: The Man Who Saved My Soul* (New York: Random House, 2004).
Holladay, William L., *The Psalms Through Three Thousand Years* (Minneapolis: Fortress Press, 1993).
Honan, Daniel J., "Newman's Poetry," in Victor R. Yanitelli, ed., *A Newman Symposium* (New York: Fordham University Press, 1952), 92–96.
Hurd, Bob, Park, Elaine and Rohrbacher, Charles, *A Contemplative Rosary* (Portland: Oregon Catholic Press, 2004).
James, P. D., *The Children of Men* (New York: A. A. Knopf, 1993).
———. *Death in Holy Orders* (New York: Ballantine Books, 2001).
Jenkins, A. Hilary, "The meaning of the Lyra Apostolica and the Genesis of 'Lead, Kindly Light,'" in G. Biemer and H. Fries, hg., *Christliche Heiligekeit als Lehre und Praxis nach John Henry Newman* (Sigmaringendorf: Verlag Glock und Lutz, 1988), 117–35.
Jeremias, Joachim, *New Testament Theology* (New York: Macmillan, 1971).
———. *The Prayers of Jesus* (London: SCM Press, 1967).
John Paul II, Pope, *Apostolic Letter on the Most Holy Rosary* (Rome: Vatican City Press, 2002).
Julian of Norwich, *Showings*, ed., Edmund Colledge and James Walsh (New York-Mahwah, NJ: Paulist Press, 1978).
Ker, Ian, *The Catholic Revival in English Literature 1845–1961* Notre Dame, IN: University of Notre Dame Press, 2003).
Kselman, "Praying the Psalms," *Church* 16 (2000), 15–17.
Küng, Hans, *Mozart, Traces of Transcendence* (Grand Rapids: Eerdmans, 1993).
Kurismmootil, Joseph K., *Heaven and Hell on Earth: An Appreciation of Five Novels of Graham Greene* (Chicago: Loyola University Press, 1982).
Lash, Nicholas, *Holiness, Speech, and Silence* (Burlington, VT and London: Ashgate Publishing, 2004).

———. "On Learning to Be Wise," *Priests and People* 15 (2001), 355–59.
Levine, Amy-Jill, *The Misunderstood Jew: The Church and the Scandal of the Jewish Jesus* (New York: HarperCollins, 2006).
Lodge, David, *Graham Greene* (New York and London: Columbia University Press, 1966).
Lubac, Henri de, *Corpus Mysticum* (Notre dame, IN: University of Notre Dame Press, 2006).
———. *The Splendor of the Church* (San Francisco: Ignatius Press, 1986).
McCabe, Herbert, *God Still Matters* (New York and London: Continuum, 2002).
McCann, J. Clinton, *A Theological Introduction to the Book of Psalms* (Nashville: Abingdon Press, 1993).
Mackey, James P., *Christianity and Creation* (New York and London: Continuum, 2006).
———. *Jesus the Man and the Myth* (New York-Ramsey: Paulist Press, 1979).
———. *Modern Theology* (New York and Oxford: Oxford University Press, 1987).
———. *The Problems of Religious Faith* (Chicago: Franciscan Herald Press, 1972).
———. "The Social Role of the Theologian," in Linda Hogan and Barbara Fitzgerald, ed., *Between Poetry and Politics* (Dublin: Columba Press, 2003), 40–53.
MacMullen, Ramsay, "The Preacher's Audience," *Journal of Theological Studies* 40 (1989), 503–11.
Macquarrie, John, "Adoration," in Gordon S. Wakefield, ed., *A Dictionary of Christian Spirituality* (London: SCM Press, 1983), 3–4.
———. *Christian Hope* (New York: The Seabury Press, 1978).
———. *Paths in Spirituality*, 2nd ed. (Harrisburg, PA: Morehouse Publishing, 1992).
Mannion, M. Francis, *Masterworks of God* (Chicago/Mundelein: Hillenbrand Books/Liturgy Training Publications, 2004).
Miller, Robert H., *Understanding Graham Greene* (Columbia, SC: University of South Carolina Press, 1990).
Moloney, Francis J., *A Body Broken for a Broken People* (Melbourne: Collins, 1990).
Moses, John, ed., *One Equal Light: An Anthology of the Writings of John Donne* (Grand Rapids: Eerdmans, 2003).
Moyaert, Paul, "In Defence of Praying with Images," *American Catholic Philosophical Quarterly* 81 (2007), 595–612.
Muir, Edwin, *An Autobiography* (St. Paul: Graywolf Press, 1990).
Murray, Alexander, "Religion Among the Poor in Thirteenth Century France: The Testimony of Humbert de Romans," *Traditio* 30 (1974), 285–324.
Newman, John H., *Historical Sketches*, vol. 2 (London: Dent, 1906).
Nichols, Aidan, "On Baptizing the Visual Arts: A Friar's Meditation on Art," *New Blackfriars* 74 (1993), 74–84.
———. *The Service of Glory* (Edinburgh: T. & T. Clark, 1997).
Nussbaum, Martha, *Poetic Justice* (Boston: Beacon Press, 1995).
O'Brien, Jim, "The Church: Circles of Grace," *The Furrow* 58 (2007), 138–44.
O'Donnell, James J., *Augustine, a New Biography* (New York: HarperCollins, 2005).
O'Donohue, John, *To Bless the Space Between Us* (New York: Doubleday, 2008).
O'Faolain, Nuala, *Are You Somebody?* (New York: Holt paperbacks, 2009).
O'Faolain, Sean, *Newman's Way* (New York: The Devin-Adair Co., 1952).
O'Meara, Thomas F., "A History of Grace," in Leo J. O'Donovan, ed., *A World of Grace* (New York: The Seabury Press, 1980), 76–91.

Pattison, George, *The End of Theology and the Task of Thinking About God* (London: SCM Press, 1998).
Preston, Geoffrey, *Faces of the Church* (Grand Rapids: Eerdmans, 1997).
Radcliffe, Timothy, *Sing a New Song: The Christian Vocation* (Springfield, IL: Templegate Publishers, 1999).
———. *What Is the Point of Being a Christian?* (New York: Continuum, 2005).
Rahner, Karl, "Theology and the Arts," *Thought* 57 (1982), 17–29.
Ratzinger, Joseph, *God and the World, A Conversation with Peter Seewald* (San Francisco: Ignatius Press, 2002).
———. *Principles of Catholic Theology* (San Francisco: Ignatius Press, 1987).
Raymo, Chet, *Climbing Brandon: Science and Faith on Ireland's Holy Mountain* (New York: Walker and Co., 2004).
Robinson, Edward, *The Language of Mystery* (London: SCM Press, 1987).
Rohlheiser, Ronald, "Knock It Off: A Challenge to Polarized Catholics," *U.S. Catholic* 72 (2007), 12–16.
Root, Howard, "Beginning All Over Again," in Alec R. Vidler, ed., *Soundings* (Cambridge: Cambridge University Press, 1962), 1–19.
Schaefer, Konrad, *Psalms* (Berit Olam Studies in Hebrew Narrative and Poetry) (Collegeville: The Liturgical Press, 2001).
Scharlemann, Robert P., *Inscriptions and Reflections: Essays in Philosophical Theology* (Charlottesville, VA: University Press of Virginia, 1989).
Scott, Kieran, "Communion in the Dark: The Cinema as Cathedral," *The Furrow* 58 (2007), 14–20.
Sharrock, Roger, "Newman's Poetry," in Ian Ker and Alan G. Hill, ed., *Newman After a Hundred Years* (Oxford: Clarendon Press, 1990), 43–61.
Simpson, E. M. and Potter, G. R., ed., *Sermons of John Donne* (Berkeley: University of California Press, 1953–1962).
Spretnak, Charlene, *Missing Mary* (New York: Palgrave-Macmillan, 2004).
Stevenson, J., ed., *A New Eusebius*, rev. ed. (London: S.P.C.K., 1987).
Stevenson, Kenneth, *Abba Father, Understanding and Using the Lord's Prayer* (Harrisburg, PA: Morehouse Publishing, 2000).
Strange, Roderick, "'A Strange Providence': Newman's Illness in Sicily," *Louvain Studies* 15 (1990), 151–65.
Sugg, Joyce, *Snapdragon: The Story of John Henry Newman* (Huntington, IN: Our Sunday Visitor, 1982).
Sylva, Dennis, *Psalms and the Transformation of Stress* (Louvain and Grand Rapids: Peeters Press and Eerdmans, 1993).
Tavard, George, *The Thousand Faces of the Virgin Mary* (Collegeville: The Liturgical Press, 1996).
Terrien, Samuel, *The Psalms* (Grand Rapids: Eerdmans, 2003).
Trevor, Meriol, *Pope John* (New York: Doubleday, 1968).
Tristram, Henry, *John Henry Newman, Autobiographical Writings* (New York: Sheed and Ward, 1957).
Tugwell, Simon, *Prayer in Practice* (Dublin: Veritas Publications, 1974).
Turner, Frank M., *John Henry Newman* (New Haven and London: Yale University Press, 2002).
United Methodist Hymnal (Nashville: United Methodist Publishing House, 1989).
Waal, Esther de, *Lost in Wonder* (Collegeville: The Liturgical Press, 2003).

———. *Seeking God: The Way of St. Benedict* (Collegeville: The Liturgical Press, 1984).
Wadell, Paul, *The Moral of the Story* (Nw York: The Crossroad Publishing Company, 2002).
Ward, J. Neville, "Contemplation," in Gordon S. Wakefield, ed., *A Dictionary of Christian Spirituality* (London: SCM Press, 1983), 95–96.
Weiser, Artur, *The Psalms* (Philadelphia: The Westminster Press, 1962).
Westerhoff, III, John W., *Will Our Children Have Faith?* (Harrisburg, PA: Morehouse Publishing, 2000).
Willimon, William H. and Hauerwas, Stanley, *Lord, Teach Us: The Lord's Prayer and the Christian Life* (Nashville: Abingdon Press, 1996).
Wood, Ralph C., "A Case for P. D. James as a Christian Novelist," *Theology Today* 59 (2002), 583–95.
———. "Deep Mysteries," *Christian Century* 117 (2000), 960–62.
———. "The Mystery of Iniquity: An Interview with P. D. James," Website of Ralph C. Wood.
———. "Rapidly Rises the Morning Tide: An Essay on P. D. James's *The Children of Men*," *Theology Today* 51 (1994).
Wright, N. T., *The Lord and His Prayer* (Grand Rapids: Eerdmans, 1996).
Young, Frances M., *From Nicaea to Chalcedon* (London: SCM Press, 1983).
———. "Mary and the Theology of Cyril of Alexandria," in William McLoughlin and Jill Pinnock, ed., *Mary for Earth and Heaven* (Leominster, UK: Gracewing, 2002), 340–54.